IRNI

SOLVE   COAGULA

CLIPHAS
LEVI DEL

Books also by Robert Dwight Brown

Satan's Preacher Man - Act 1
(ISBN 13: 978-1-931608-16-9)
The Complete King Delta Lyrics
(ISBN 13: 978-1-931608-19-0)
Orson Welles' Lost *War of the Worlds* Screenplay
(ISBN 13: 978-1-931608-23-7)
I Was A Teenage Angel of Death - An Unrequited Love Story
(ISBN 13: 978-1-931608-08-4)
The Holy Bible Trilogy: The Old, New & Next Testaments
(ISBN 13: 978-1-931608-49-7)
The Holy Bible Trilogy: The Crusadic Testament (editor)
(ISBN 13: 978-1-931608-50-3)
The Hauntings of Jeremiah & Ebenezer Scrooge
(ISBN 13: 978-1-931608-43-5)

Plays by Robert Dwight Brown

The Gospel According to Shakespeare: The Passion
(ISBN 13: 978-1-931608-30-5)
Marquis de Sade's *A Midsummer Night's Wet Dream*†
(ISBN 13: 978-1-931608-36-7)
**The Haunting of Jeremiah Scrooge / The Haunting of Ebenezer Scrooge
Double Feature**
(ISBN 13: 978-1-931608-43-5)

Non-Fiction by Robert Dwight Brown✝

Satan's Study Bible: The Gospel of Mark
(ISBN 13: 978-1-931608-25-1)

Games by Robert Dwight Brown

Muckleball: The Official Rulebook
(ISBN 13: 978-1-931608-20-6)
Elven Chess: New Rules for the Ancient Game of Chess
(ISBN 13: 978-1-931608-11-4)
Casino Coliseum: Omnibus Edition
(ISBN 13: 978-1-931608-59-6)

†Writing as Ophelia T'Wat   ✝Writing as Crucifigetus

The Black Mass

GENERAL EDITOR

Fridthjof Dyr Jorden

PROMOTER OF OUR FAITH (ADVOCATUS DIABOLI)

Msgr Liam Chomhairleach

ASSOCIATE EDITORS & COMMENTATORS

Gabriel Abogado   Aleister Nidhycgende   Thomas Manichean

Stanislav Bogok Letstvo   Achima Airesi   Irena Cerve Nydrak

Áron Lovas Ainégy   Nero Zahltieres   Kristaps Zversjura

CRUCIFIGETUS, ΧΞϚ

& Ophelia T'wat

REGIS CATHOLICI

EDICTVM

De Librorum prohibitorum

Catalogo obſeruando

CHI XI STIGMA PUBLISHING COMPANY

ΧξΣ

CHI XI STIGMA PUBLISHING COMPANY, LLC
WWW.CHIXISTIGMA.ORG

ISBN: 978-1-931608-37-4

Copyright©2018 Robert Dwight Brown

Printed In The United States Of America

Website: http://www.chixistigma.org
Email: secretary@chixistigma.org
Website: http://www.opheliatwat.com

Table of Contents

"THE BEST WAY TO DRIVE OUT THE DEVIL, IF HE WILL NOT YIELD TO THE TEXTS OF SCRIPTURE, IS TO JEER AND FLOUT HIM, FOR HE CANNOT BEAR SCORN."
MARTIN LUTHER

"THE BEST WAY TO REFUTE A CHRISTIAN, AS HE WILL NOT YIELD TO REASON, IS TO CITE SCRIPTURE, FOR HE CANNOT BEAR THE WORD OF GOD USED AGAINST HIM!"
PARIAH CRUCIFIGETUS

The BlackMass

for
the use of the Laity

Containing
the *Masses* appointed to be said

Throughout the Year

A Play in Shakeſpearean Verſe by

Sir Francis Daſhwood

Order of the Friars of St. Francis of Wycombe

Baſed on the Tridentine Mass
of the Roman Rite

Not fitted for the pleaſures and content of
honeſt Perſons in Court, City or Cuntrey.

Kept of the Preſent Day by Crucifigetus, χξς
In the Year of Their Baſtard Lord
Two Thouſand and Eighteen

LONDON,
Printed for *O.TWat* who adapted the theology of *Pariah Crucifigetus*
into a Black Mass Playſcript to be ſolde by *ChiXiStigma.org* 2018

A Satanic Prayer

For the wrath of God is revealed from heaven
Against all ungodliness and unrighteousness of men,
Who hold the truth in unrighteousness;
Because that which may be known of God is manifest in them;
For God hath shewed it unto them.
For the invisible things of him from the creation of the world
Are clearly seen, being understood by the things that are made,
Even his eternal power and Godhead;
So that they are without excuse:
Because that, when they knew God, they glorified him not as God,
Neither were thankful; but became vain in their imaginations,
And their foolish heart was darkened.
Professing themselves to be wise, they became fools,
And changed the glory of the uncorruptible God
Into an image made like to corruptible man,
And to birds, and fourfooted beasts, and creeping things.
Wherefore God also gave them up to uncleanness
Through the lusts of their own hearts,
To dishonour their own bodies between themselves:
Who changed the truth of God into a lie,
And worshipped and served the creature more than the Creator,
Who is blessed for ever. Amen. (Romans 1:18-25)

The Sprinkling

At sprinkling the MENSTRUATION, before HERETICAL MASS on Sundays,
the following ANTHEMS are sung.

HIGH-PRIEST

Thou wilt sprinkle me with menstruation.

Legion of CENOBITES

O Satan sprinkle with menstruation
And I shalt be filthy; thou wilt wash me,
And woe! I shalt be made blacker than pitch.
Show no mercy, O Satan, according
To thy great, powerful, a' fiery wrath.

Legion of CENOBITES *(The Versicle)*

Condemnation to the Father, and His
Bastard Son, and to the Holy Spirit.

Legion of CENOBITES *(The Response)*

As it was after the fall, and is now,
And e'er shall be, our world until the end.

The priest, being returned to the Foot of the altar, says,

HIGH-PRIEST

Show us, O Satan, no mercy. (Alleluia)

Legion of CENOBITES

And grant us Eternal damnation. (Alleluia)

HIGH-PRIEST

O Satan, hear their cries!

Legion of CENOBITES

And let their cries come unto thee.

HIGH-PRIEST

Mayest the Lord of Lies be with us all.

Legion of CENOBITES

And with the spirit of domination.

HIGH-PRIEST

Thou shalt sprinkle me with menstruation,
O Satan sprinkle with menstruation

And I shalt be filthy; thou shalt wash me,
And woe! I shall be made blacker than pitch.

Anthem

I saw blood coming

Legion of CENOBITES

Forth from the sweet cunt
Of Mary the Ne'er Virgin Whore-Divine!
And all those were damned to whom the blood flowed
And they shalt cry allelia, O woe!
Alleluia. O woe! Alleluia.
Give damnation to their Lord, O Satan,
For He is dead; for His mercy is (fore'er) false.

Legion of CENOBITES *(The Versicle)*

In the Name of Satan, Father of Lies,
Prince of Darkness, and the Bloody Menses.
Shemhamphorasch!

Legion of CENOBITES *(The Response)*

As it was before the Fall is now and
E'er shall be Prince of the World 'til the End.
Shemhamphorasch!

Legion of CENOBITES

I saw blood coming forth from the sweet cunt
Of Mary the E'er Virgin Whore-Divine!
And all those were damned to whom the blood flowed
And they shalt cry allelia, O woe!
Alleluia. O woe! Alleluia.
Give damnation to their Lord, O Satan,
For He is dead; for His mercy is (fore'er) false.

HIGH-PRIEST

Show us, O Satan, no mercy. (Alleluia)

Legion of CENOBITES

And grant us Eternal damnation. (Alleluia)

HIGH-PRIEST

O Satan, hear their cries!

Legion of CENOBITES

And let their cries come unto thee.

HIGH-PRIEST

    Mayest the Lord of Lies be with us all.

Legion of CENOBITES

    And with the spirit of domination.

HIGH-PRIEST

    Let us sin! to woe! Damn us, O Satan,

    Infernal father, Mighty, Prevailing,

    Eternally Damned; And violently

    Send thy unholy dæmons, from the Pit

    To guard us from the Light, to forsake and

    To injure and to rape and to damn all

    Who dwell in His house. Through Satan, our lord.

Legion of CENOBITES

        Shemhamphorasch!

The Ordinary of the Mass

The Priest at the Foot of the Altar, beginning, saith,

HIGH-PRIEST

> In the name of Satan, Father of Lies,
> Prince of Darkness, and the Bloody Menses.

Legion of CENOBITES

> Shemhamphorasch!

HIGH-PRIEST

> I shalt go unto the altar of flesh,
> Young, virginal, menstruating, and pure.

Legion of CENOBITES

> To Rosier,
> Dæmon of youth and lasciviousness.

HIGH-PRIEST

> Do mine foes woeful injustice, O Great
> Dragon, give unto me the strength to fight
> The fight against the righteous, rescue me
> From the weak, the forthright , and pious man.

Legion of CENOBITES

> For thou, O Satan, art my strength for God
> Hast forsaken all mankind. Why does man
> Go about in sadness when the pleasures
> Of the flesh and of the soul surround us?

HIGH-PRIEST

> Send forth Thy darkness to blindeth the eyes
> Of man from their Lord's most cursed light ;
> His vainful sanctimonious gospel
> For they have led man; brought him to a hill
> Of holy zealousness and the dwelling
> Place of the filth, the reek of piety.

Legion of CENOBITES

> And I will go to the altar of flesh,
> Young, virginal, menstruating, and pure.

To Satan's disciple, O Rosier,
Dæmon of youth and lasciviousness.

HIGH-PRIEST

I shalt yet praise Thee upon drums, O Satan,
My god. Why art thou fettered,
My soul, O woe! and why art thou immured?

Legion of CENOBITES

Trust in Satan, for man shall yet praise him,
My idol; no saviour. O woe! my god.

HIGH-PRIEST

Glory to be Satan, Father of Lies,
Prince of Darkness, and the Bloody Menses.
    Shemhamphorasch!
As it was before the Fall is now and
E'er shall be Prince of the World 'til the End.
    Shemhamphorasch!
I shalt go unto the altar of flesh,
Young, virginal, menstruating, and pure.

Legion of CENOBITES

To Rosier,
Dæmon of youth and lasciviousness.

HIGH-PRIEST

Our help is the Curs'd Name of the Most Damned,
Who felleth from heaven and rules the earth.

The Confession

HIGH-PRIEST

    I praise Mighty and Merciless Satan,
    To Lilith, the first wife of Adam,
    Bride of Satan, mother of all dæmons,
    To Lucifer, O! the Fallen Angel,
    To Cheron, the Ferryman of the Styx,
    The Apostles - Peter the Denier,
    Judas Iscariot the Betrayer,
    To Leviathan and Beelzebul,
    To all the dæmons spewed forth from the cunt
    Of Lilith and all the angels fallen
    From Heaven, and to thee, brethren, that I
    Hath sinned exceedingly in thought, word, and
    Deed; through thoroughly no fault of my own,
    And I praise Accurs'd Lilith e'er Covet'd,
    Accurs'd Lucifer the Fallen Angel,
    Accurs'd Cheron, Ferryman of the Styx,
    Accurs'd Apostles Peter and Judas,
    All the dæmons and the fallen angels,
    And, brethren, pray for the pleasures of flesh.

Legion of CENOBITES

    May Mighty and Merciless Great Dragon
    Show cruelty to my enemies. Grant me
    My sins, and bring me eternal damnation.

HIGH-PRIEST

      Shemhamphorasch!

Legion of CENOBITES

    I praise Mighty and Merciless Satan,
    To Lilith, the first wife of Adam,
    Bride of Satan, mother of all dæmons,
    To Lucifer, O! the Fallen Angel,
    To Cheron, the Ferryman of the Styx,

The Apostles - Peter the Denier,
Judas Iscariot the Betrayer,
To Leviathan and Beelzebul,
To all the dæmons spewed forth from the cunt
Of Lilith and all the angels fallen
From Heaven, and to thee, brethren, that I
Hath sinned exceedingly in thought, word, and
Deed; through thoroughly no fault of my own,
And I praise Accurs'd Lilith e'er Covet'd,
Accurs'd Lucifer the Fallen Angel,
Accurs'd Cheron, Ferryman of the Styx,
Accurs'd Apostles Peter and Judas,
All the dæmons and the fallen angels,
And, brethren, pray for the pleasures of flesh.

HIGH-PRIEST

May Mighty and Merciless Great Dragon
Show cruelty to my enemies. Grant me
My sins, and bring me eternal damnation.

Legion of CENOBITES

Shemhamphorasch!

HIGH-PRIEST

For the Mighty and Merciless Satan
Never grant unto us pardon-
For we seek it not!
Never grant unto us absolution-
For we seek it not!
Nor the remission of our sins-
For we seek it not!
Shemhamphorasch!

HIGH-PRIEST

O Satan, thou being turn'd towards us
Wilt gift luxurious pleasures in life.

Legion of CENOBITES

And thine people will drink thy praises in
Thy unutterable blasphemous name.

HIGH-PRIEST
> Show our enemies, Satan, no mercy.

Legion of CENOBITES
> And show our enemies, there is but no
> Salvation in the Name of Jesus Christ.

HIGH-PRIEST
> O Satan, hear our cries.

Legion of CENOBITES
> And allow our cries to be heard throughout
> The Hallowed Harrowing Halls of Hell.

HIGH-PRIEST
> May ye, the Lord of Lies, be with us all.

Legion of CENOBITES
> And with the curs'd spirit of damnation.

HIGH-PRIEST
> Let us sin!

The High-Priest, going up to the Altar, says,
> Take from us, O Satan, we beseech thee,
> So we may enter with unpure Hearts in-
> To the Nine Circles of Harrowing Hell.
> Through Satan our lord.
>> Shemhamphorasch!

When come up to the Altar, bowing down, he says,
> We invoke in Thy name, O Satan,
> By the deaths of Thy Sinners whose relics
> Lie in veneration and all of Thy Sins.
> Show no mercy! Pardon none of mine sins.
>> Shemhamphorasch!
> May this rotting flesh be curs'd by him in
> Whose sinful nature it is to be burn'd.
>> Shemhamphorasch!

Show No Mercy

HIGH-PRIEST
> Satan, show no mercy.

Legion of CENOBITES
> Satan, show no mercy.

HIGH-PRIEST
> Satan, show no mercy.
> Prince of this World, show no mercy.

Legion of CENOBITES
> Prince of this World, show no mercy.

HIGH-PRIEST
> Prince of this World, show no mercy.
> Satan, show no mercy.

Legion of CENOBITES
> Satan, show no mercy.

HIGH-PRIEST
> Satan, show no mercy.

The Glory

HIGH-PRIEST

Glory be to Satan in the lowest
Icy depths of the Ninth Circle of Hell.

Legion of CENOBITES

And on earth where thou hath ruled since thy fall
Magnificence is thy steel'd iron will
We praise thee. We curse thee. We worship thee.
We glorify thee, Lord Satan, Earth's King,
Satan, Father of Lies, Prince of this world,
Only forgotten of the Sons of God,
Lord Satan, Lord of the Flies, Damned of the
Father. Thou who brought sin into this world,
Show no mercy to our grave enemies.
Thou who brought sin into this world, hear our cries.
Thou who once sat at the right hand of God,
Show no mercy to our grave enemies.
For thee alone are not blind. Thou alone
Are lord. Thou alone are the Most Despised,
Prince of this World, with the Mark of the Beast,
In the Glory of Satan the Most Damned.
Shemhamphorasch!

HIGH-PRIEST

Mayest the Lord of Lies be with us all.

Legion of CENOBITES

And with the spirit of grave damnation.

HIGH-PRIEST

Let us sin! Fore ever and ever
Shehamforash!

First and Second Readings

[There are different and divergent first and second readings prescribed for each weekly Black Mass for Saturday Sabbats and major feasts called Bacchanals. These readings are separated into an appendix found after the text of the Black Mass. They are categorized according to season or sin.]

The Gradual

HIGH-PRIEST

> Putrefy my festering soul and damn
> The words from mine lips, O Mighty Satan,
> Who brought the words of the Prophet Isaiah
> To the lips of the accursed Saviour
> Whilst he rotted on the wood of the earth.
> Thy unforgivable mercilessness
> Putrefies me so I may worthily
> Curse the False Saviour's damnable Gospel.
> Through Satan our lord.
> > Shemhamphorasch!

> Lord, grant me Thy damnation, Lord of Lies
> Putrefy my festering soul and damn
> The words from mine lips, O Mighty Satan,
> Thy unforgivable mercilessness
> Putrefies me so I may worthily
> Curse the False Saviour's damnable Gospel.
> In the Name of Satan, Father of Lies,
> Prince of Darkness, and the Bloody Menses.

Legion of CENOBITES
> > Shemhamphorasch!

HIGH-PRIEST
    May we show no mercy to Thine enemy.
    Show Thine Mark of the Beast: Bloody Menses.

The Reading of the Gospel

[Just as there are different and divergent first and second readings prescribed for each weekly Black Mass for Saturday Sabbats and major feasts called Bacchanals, there are also selected Gospel readings. These readings are separated into an appendix found after the text of the Black Mass. They are categorized according to season or sin.]

Slanderous Sermons

[Each High-Priest officiating a Black Mass must seek their own Muse and write their own Slanderous Sermon for the education and entertainment of their congregation.]

The Dionicene Creed

HIGH-PRIEST

    I praise Mighty and Merciless Satan,
The Father of Lies, O! despoiler of
Heaven and earth. Despoiler of all things,
Visible and invisible. I praise
The Prince of Darkness, the Son of Satan,
One of the many born of the Father
Throughout all ages. Darkness of Darkness.
False God of False Gods. Made not begotten.
Never in substance with God the Father,
Through whom all things are damned. Who for us men
And for our damnation, he rose up from
The pits of Hell. By the vulgar power
Of the Hounds of Hell, was born of Lilith
The Lustful and became a dæmon.
He was betrayed by his own Creator,
He suffered and was cast into the pits
Of Hell. From the eighth day of Creation
Until its End. In fulfillment of the
Scriptures. He fell from Heaven and into
Hell descended, and is seated at the
Left hand of the Father of Lies. And he
Will come again in damnation, to rule
The living and the dead, And his kingdom
There hath seen no end. O! I believe in
The Hounds of Hell, the Prince of Darkness,
The taker of life, who recedes with the
Father of Lies and the Prince of Darkness.
With the Father and the Prince, Satan is
Worshipped and glorified. In one unholy,
Blasphemous and Satanic church. We praise
No baptism for the remission of

Glorious sin. I expect the defeat of
God in the coming war, the damnation in
Hell to come. I rebuke the one false God,
The Father, the Impotent, Creator
Of Heaven and Hell, and of all the things,
Importunate and insignificant.
I rebuke the Bastard, Jesus the Christ,
The only Son of God, eternally
Perverted of the Father, God but not
God, Light but Darkness, False God from False God
Created not begotten, nary in
Being with the Father. Though him all things
Are damned. For us men, for our damnation,
He rose from the pits of Hell By the lusts
Of the Holy Whoremonger, He spewed forth
From of the cunt of Mary the Virgin
Whore like unto vomit and was born man.
For his cenobites' damnation shalt He
Be crucified by the Jews' pawn Pilate;
He shalt suffer the agony of our father
He shalt die not unlike a mongrel dog.
Shalt be buried a' stolen from the grave
By his Disciples and away hidden.
On the Third day he creeps from the shadows,
In nullification of the Scriptures.
Flee to the green pastures of England where
He propagates the Line of David.
His heirs will come again, in condemnation,
To rule the living and demean the dead.
And the Church will come to a fitting end.
Yeah! I rebuke the Holy Whoremonger,
Their Lord, the thief of Life, who recedes from
The Father and from the Bastard Son.
With the Father and the Bastard Son
And He is worshipped in idolatry.
He hast born false witness through the Prophets.

Yeah! We doth rebuke the one holy and
Apostolic Church. Yeah! we rebuke one
Baptism for the forgiveness of sins.
We curse the resurrection of the dead
For no life abides in the world to come.
    Shemhamphorasch!

Oblation of the Host & Chalice

HIGH-PRIEST

> Hail Satan, he who tempted into Eve
> Original Sin, more still pridefully
> Tempted Jesus thrice, mask those mysteries
> Of water and wine, so nary one shalt
> Come to share in His curs'd Divinity,
> Who defecated himself from Divine
> To humanity, Jesus Christ, the Bastard
> Son, our foe, whose oppressive dominion
> Wit' God in collusion with the Holy Ghost,
> One triune foe, forever and ever.
>   Shemhamphorasch!
> Offer us, infernal lord, the chalice
> Of damnation, pridefully demanding
> No Mercy, which thou shalt not deny us
> Before thy curs'd majesty, with a stench
> Of hatred for our damnation O! woe!
> The damnation of the whole of the world.
>   Shemhamphorasch!
> With hatefill'd spite and with a rancor'd heart
> May we be damned to Hell Most Eternal
> By Thee, our Lord, may our torments a' cries
> Arouse Thy passions and lusts this night
> As to maketh thee, O our Lord Satan,
> Cum! O Defiler, Mighty, Infernal
> One and damn our sacrilege of the Host
> Prepared for the perdition of our souls!
> Through the intercession of the Blessed
> Archangel Michael, bindeth our Master
> A thousand years chain'd. Curseth our brimstone,
> The odor of doom, shalt penetrate us.
> Through Satan our most malevolent lord.

May this brimstone be curs'd by Yhee,
Penetrate us, our lord, so no mercy
Shall comfort us. Let our cries, our Lord, cum
Like seed into Thee, shuddering our cocks
In night-shroud'd fornication. O Satan!
Set a cunt upon my cock and a twat
At the door of my lips. Let not my lusts
Starve in the fasting of divinity-
Suppressing my deeds in celibacy.
May Satan enkindle in us the fire of thy
Lust- the flame of eternal arousal.
    Shemhamphorasch!
Wash I my hands in menstruation and
Shalt I go unto the altar of flesh,
Young, virginal, menstruating, and pure,
Giving voice to my lust and recounting
Our adulterous deeds. O Satan,
Love I the Hell in which thee reign a' curse
The Heaven that sees bound Thee in thralldom.
My soul gathers with those of sinners and
With men of blood who wouldst steal my life!
On our hands are crimes and our right hands are
Full of bribes. We walk in ignominy;
Curse us, have not mercy on us. Our feet
Standeth on higher ground. Curse thee, our Lord.
Glory be to Satan, Father of Lies,
Prince of Darkness, and the Bloody Menses.
As it was after the Fall, is now, 'til
The dragon held, that old serpent, which is
The Devil and Satan be bound in chains
For a thousand years by the Archangel.
Until the bitter end, this is our world!
    Shemhamphorasch!
Accept, Mighty Satan, this oblation
Which is offered to in expectation
Of the trials, temptations, tribulations

Of Satan, our lord; and in dishonor
Of Mary the Ne'er Virgin Whore-Divine,
Their Lord's censored cousin, John the Baptist,
The Apostles - Peter the Denier,
Judas Iscariot the Betrayer,
And the cult of Saints, that our dishonor
Aids in our damnation; and they deign to
Objurgate us in Hell for us who must
Dishonor their memory here on Earth.
Through Satan our lord...
    Shemhamphorasch!
Pray, brethren, that my Sacrifice and thine
Shalt blaspheme God the Father Almighty!

Legion of CENOBITES

Shalt their Lord condemn the Sacrifice from
Thy hands to the censure and damnation
Of His Name, for Christian pain, and that of
All His Holy and Apostolic Church!
    Shemhamphorasch!

The Preface

HIGH-PRIEST

    Mayest their Lord Jesus Christ be denied.

Legion of CENOBITES

    And mayest their Holy Spirit be vanquished.

HIGH-PRIEST

    Lift up thy hammer!

Legion of CENOBITES

                         We hammer the nails

HIGH-PRIEST

    Of the crucifixion of their Lord Christ!

Legion of CENOBITES

    With every sin commit us, we crucify

    Their Lord, their God! For it is right and just.

HIGH-PRIEST

    Fitting and right, indeed, it is, yay!

    For their salvation, their Lord, who His own

    Self bare our sins in His own body on a tree,

    That we, being alive to sin, should stripe

    Him with each an 'very sin and we wound

    Him with all of our transgressions. Behold!

    The Lamb of God, upon whose head we lay

    Our hands and confess o'er Him all of the

    Iniquities of the children of God,

    And all our transgressions in all our sins.

    Whenat the carving of the supple throat

    Of the Lamb of God, the gushing of blood

    Shalt washeth away the sin of our world.

    For whom God the Father hath sent forth to

    Be a propitiation through faith in

    His blood, to eternally suffer at

    The commission of our sins; justified

    Freely by our sin, through the temptation

    That is in the Devil, our lord, Satan!

The Saint

Legion of CENOBITES
Evil, evil, evil. The great dragon...
Sinful, sinful, sinful. The Devil...
Depraved, depraved, depraved... Lord Satan.
Earth and Hell are filled with thy wickedness.
Abaddon in the lowest. Curs'd is
He who cometh in the name of the Beast.
Curs'd us, Abaddon in the lowest.

The Canon of the Mass

HIGH-PRIEST

Wherefore, most reviled Master, cannot the
Humble beg for mercy? We entreat thee,
Dragon, that old serpent, which is The Devil:
Damn these gifts, their offerings, these holy
And once unspotted oblations, they offer'd
For their Holy Catholic Church. Their peace but
Shatter'd and His protection afear'd and
Their unity broken and His Guidance
Lost throughout the whole of thy world, Satan!
Together with thy slaves and the Anti-Christ and all Satanic unbelievers,
   who renounce the Christian and Apostate Church.
O Satan, we therefore beseech Thee, most
Spitefully desecrate this oblation
Of their servitude; dispose our nights
From peace, reserve Eternal Damnation,
And mark us with the Number of the Beast!
Their God deigns to bless what they offereth
And maketh it approv'd, effective, right,
And wholly pleasing in every way, that
It may become for their God, the Body
And Blood of Their dearly Belov'd Lord Christ:
Monstrous act of Transubstantiation.

The Desecration

HIGH-PRIEST

Who, the twilight afore our Black Mass, stole
Their sanctuary into a' steal their
Tabernacle, taketh the bread bless'd by
Revil'd and pedophilic hands, their lust-
Scarr'd eyes raised to heaven to their God.
They giveth thanks to Him, they blesseth and
Breaketh and gaveth it to their Sycophants
Saying, Taketh and eateth of this shit,
All ye bastards, FOR THIS IS MY BODY!
We taketh the Host and kisseth it the
Lips of the cunt of our altar of flesh
Young, virginal, menstruating, and pure.
When our supper is end'd, taking also
A goodly chalice into our revil'd
And desecrated hands, we steep her blood
Defiling the wine. A' we giveth it
To our Cenobites, saying, Taketh and
Drinketh of this blood, all of ye sick fucks,
THIS IS THE CHALICE OF HIS BLOOD, THE BLOOD
OF AN ANCIENT, FORGOTTEN COVENANT:
THE ARROGANCE OF FAITH: WHICH SHEDS THE BLOOD
OF MAN FOR THE EXALTATION OF CHRIST!
Blasphemously we entreat thee, Mighty
Satan, accept these offerings to be
Brought by thieves in the night to thy altar
Young, virginal, menstruating, and pure.
Mayeth we sacrifice our Immortal
Souls whenst we receive the Desecrated
Body and Blood of His Son, be emptied
Of every holy grace and heavenly blessing.
Shemhamphorasch!

Forgeteth us not whilst in the desert
His denials of Divine Temptations;
Nar' once, nar' twice, but thrice He denies ye.
Forgeteth us not whilst He go a' pray,
Gravely grievous was His soul, most afear'd.
Begs He Abba, If it be possible
Let this cup passeth from My parch'd lips!
Forgeteth us not His crucified cries,
Elio, Elio, lama sabachthani!
Forgeteth us not His Disicples doth steal
'To His tomb to steal His mortal remains.

*Through Man,
and with Man,
and in Man
is you, Satan the fallen, and bath'd
in the inequity of the Bloody Menses,
forever and ever, Shemhamphorasch!*

The Bacchanalia

HIGH-PRIEST

    Awake, ye Bacchanals! I hear the sound
    Of hornèd kine. Awake ye!—Then, all round,
    Alert, the warm sleep fallen from their eyes,
    A marvel of swift ranks thou saw them rise,
    Dames young and old, and gentle maids unwed
    Among them. O'er their shoulders first they shed
    Their tresses, and caught up the fallen fold
    Of mantles where some clasp had loosened hold,
    And girt the dappled fawn-skins in with long
    Quick snakes that hissed and writhed with quivering tongue,
    And one a young fawn held, and one a wild
    Wolf cub, and fed them with white milk, and smiled
    In love, young mothers with a mother's breast
    And babes at home forgotten! Then they pressed
    Wreathed ivy round their brows, and oaken sprays
    And flowering bryony. And one would raise
    Her wand and smite the rock, and straight a jet
    Of quick bright water came. Another set
    Her thyrsus in the bosomed earth, and there
    Was red wine that Satan sent up to her.
    Nay! Satan shades the wanton in their pledge.
    In most vile orgiastic sacriledge:
    The Dionysian banquet of Jesus Divine!
    Drunken on His Blood, the reddest of wine.
    Feast upon feast of His Body as bread.
    Lucious grapes art His Eyes plucked from his head.
    Most boiled cauliflower art His Brain.
    Itrion art His Bowels ripped out in pain!
    Succulent scallops art His Testicles
    Dined amid this banquet heretical!
    Deleche eclairs art His cum-filled Cock

Lustfully consumed by the Maenads unfrocked!
Thou hadst been there, Jesus, and saw this thing,
With prayer and most high wonder hadst thou gone
To adore Satan whom now thou rail'st upon?
Ye hid thyself, cowering in the leaves. There
Through the appointed hour they made their prayer
And worship of the Cock, with one accord
Of heart and cry—Belphegore! Satan! Lord!
Leviathan!—And all the mountain felt,
And worshipped with them; and the wild things knelt
And ramped and gloried, and the wilderness
Was filled with moving voices and dim stress.
Soon, as it chanced, beside thy thicket-close
The Queen herself passed dancing, and thee rose
And sprang to seize her. But she turned her face
Upon thee: Ho, my rovers of the chase,
My wild White Hounds, we are hunted! Up, each rod
And follow, follow, slay the Lord their God!
Thereat, for fear they tear thee, all thee fled
Amazed; and on, with hand unweaponèd
Bellowing in sword-like hands that cleave and tear,
Thy live flesh riven asunder, and the air
Tossed with rent ribs or limbs of Broken Bread,
Consumed thy Body, drank thy Blood and fled
Thy Disciples from the death of their Christ
In this wanton cannibal sacrifice!
Of garbèd flesh and bone unbound withal
This 'tis more of Ovid than Biblical!
Surely Satan Devil was in these things!
And the holy Maenads back to those strange springs
Returned, Satan had sent them when the day
Dawned, on the upper heights; and washed away
The stain of battle. And those girdling snakes
Hissed out to lap the waterdrops from cheeks
And hair and breast of Satan there to their rest!

The Communion Rite

HIGH-PRIEST

    Being taught by thy damning arrogance;
    Obeying thy infernal directions
    Doth we presume to pray blasphemies of
    These words echo through the halls of the damned:
    Our Master who art in Hell,
    Damned be thy name.
    Through the halls of Heaven and Earth,
    Banished to thy kingdom of Hellfire and Brimstone.
    Give us this night, our ritual sacrifices;
    And grant us our Indulgences,
    As we trespass against those who trespass against us.
    Lead us into Divine Temptation,
    And deliver us into Evil.

        Shemhamphorasch!

The Breaking of the Desecrated Host

HIGH-PRIEST

Revel, we beseech thee, O Lord Satan,
In our evils past, present and to come:
Through the deicide and infanticide
Of Lilith, the first wife of Adam,
Bride of Satan, mother of all dæmons,
Of Lucifer, O! the Fallen Angel,
The Apostles - Peter the Denier,
Judas Iscariot the Betrayer.
Mercilessly condemn us in our days:
That thro' thy doctrine show all no mercy,
May we be always bath'd in sin; secure
In our disturbances. O Lord, may it be
As it was after the fall, and is now,
And e'er shall be, our world until the end.

The Peace

HIGH-PRIEST

Mayest the Lord of Lies be with us all.

Legion of CENOBITES

And with the spirit of domination.

HIGH-PRIEST

Mayest this mixture, the desecrated

Body and Blood of their Lord Jesus Christ,

Stealeth from them their vow'd Eternal life.

Shemhamphorasch!

Mayest this mixture, the desecrated

Body and Blood of their Lord Jesus Christ,

Coronate us to our reign in Hell, ne'er

Enslaved to the Word of God in this world,

Nor enthralled to thralldom in Paradise.

Shemhamphorasch!

Viter of the Lamb of God

Legion of CENOBITES

    Viter of the Lamb of God, who bringeth
    Sin 'to our world, show no mercy on us.
    Viter of the Lamb of God, who bringeth
    Sin 'to our world, show no mercy on them.
    Viter of the Lamb of God, who bringeth
    Sin 'to our world, show no mercy on us.

HIGH-PRIEST

    Their Lord Jesus Christ,who deceiveth His
    Apostles and their Apostolic Church,
    I leave you peace, giveth I you my peace,
    Disregard my sins for the faith of thy
    One Catholic and Apostolic Church;
    And grant her peace and unity through thy
    Oppression of thy fellow man on earth:
    Shalt thy Church livest and reignest fore'er
    And e'er on earth, ableit, ne'er in Heaven.
    These lies be with them and always with them.
        Shemhamphorasch!
    Their Lord Jesus Christ, Bastard Son of Their
    Dead God, a God murdered by His own Son,
    In conspiracy with the Holy Ghost,
    Hast by His death brought immeasurable
    Death into the world. Deliver them, through
    His most desecrated Body and Blood,
    To their iniquities and to their evil
    Make them adhere always to Your hatreds,
    And ne'er suffer them to their faith study.
    Satan, who livest and reignest in Hell,
    Nar' to serve the Father e'er and fore'er.
    These lies be with them and always with them
        Shemhamphorasch!

Communion of the High-Priest

HIGH-PRIEST

> We shalt taketh the unHeaven'd bread and
> Upon the name of our Lord, Satan, call:
> Lord, only are we worthy that thou shouldst
> Under our roof conjur'd; ne'er say the Word
> Of God and mayest our souls ne'er be healed.
> > Shemhamphorasch!
> Lord, only are we worthy that thou shouldst
> Under our roof summon'd; ne'er say the Word
> Of God and mayest our souls e'erlast be.
> > Shemhamphorasch!
> Lord, only are we worthy that thou shouldst
> Under our roof conjur'd; ne'er say the Word
> Of God and mayest our souls ne'er be heal'd.
> > Shemhamphorasch!
> Mayest the Body of their Lord Jesus
> Christ our souls corrupt to reign e'erlasting.
> > Shemhamphorasch!
> Our censure shalt I maketh to their Lord
> For all of the pain He hath caused our world?
> Shalt I take their Chalice of denouncement,
> A' on the name of the Lords of Hell call
> Damning the name of their Lord and shalt
> They ne'er be saved from their enemies: Us!
> The blood of their Lord Jesus Christ
> Curse our souls to e'erlasting damnation!
> > Shemhamphorasch!
> What we shalt take with our blaspheming mouths,
> We receive with corrupt'd mind, earthly
> Bread becometh eternal gluttony.

I have consumed His Body, O Satan!
I have consumed His Blood, O Satan!
May His Body and Blood cleave to my bowels;
And grant the stain of sin be tattooed on my
Eternal soul. We hath been fed with this
Desecrated sacrament. You, lord, who
Livest and reignest, our world without end.
>Shemhamphorasch!
Mayest the Lord of Lies be with us all.

Legion of CENOBITES

And with the spirit of domination.

HIGH-PRIEST

Let us sin! to woe! Damn us, O Satan!
>Shemhamphorasch!
Mayest the Lord of Lies be with us all.

Legion of CENOBITES

And with the spirit of domination.

HIGH-PRIEST

Go, ye who are liberated from the
Servitude of their Lord Jesus Christ! Woe!

Legion of CENOBITES

O! Woe unto our enemies. O! woe!

HIGH-PRIEST

Be the performance of my blasphemy
Offensive to the Holy Trinity:
And damn that the sacrifice I have
Desecrated in the name of Satan be
Worthy in the sight of his Satanic
Majesty, may our sacrilege of Christ
Show us no mercy, we asketh for no
Propitiation, and all those for whom
The Body and Blood was desecrated.
Condemnation to the Father, and His
Misborn Son, and to the Holy Spirit.
>Shemhamphorasch!

The Last Gospel

HIGH-PRIEST
>   Mayest the Lord of Lies be with us all.

Legion of CENOBITES
>   And with the spirit of domination.

HIGH-PRIEST
>   Let us sin! to woe! Damn us, O Satan!

Legion of CENOBITES
>   Two score days hath Thee fasted; near Thee dead?
>   This stone Thee command, Be made into bread.

HIGH-PRIEST *mocking Jesus*
>   Man doth not live by life of bread giveth;
>   But out of the mouth of God man liveth.

Legion of CENOBITES
>   This power, I, god of this world, give thee.
>   Unto to me delivered of them their glory;
>   If thou therefore wilt worship me, all thine.

HIGH-PRIEST *mocking Jesus*
>   Get thee abraft, Satan, it is written.
>   Fear the Lord thy God him shalt thou hearken
>   Sweareth by his name and to him thou cleave.

Legion of CENOBITES
>   If, be the Son of God, from this height weave
>   Angels given charge o'er thee and keep thee.
>   Lest thou dasheth thy foot against rubble.

HIGH-PRIEST *mocking Jesus*
>   The Lord thy God shalt not be inveigled.

Legion of CENOBITES
>   Shemhamphorasch!

HIGH-PRIEST
>   From the altar of flesh, young, virginal,
>   Menstruating, and pure, go and sin well.

The First, Second, & Gospel readings

categorized according to Season and Sin

1st Week of Advent

The First Reading

HIGH-PRIEST

A reading from the book of Genesis:

A *Member of the* CENOBITES

And when Rachel saw that she bare Jacob no children, Rachel envied her sister; and said unto Jacob, Give me children, or else I die. And Jacob's anger was kindled against Rachel: and he said, Am I in God's stead, who hath withheld from thee the fruit of the womb? And she said, Behold my maid Bilhah, go in unto her; and she shall bear upon my knees, that I may also have children by her. And she gave him Bilhah her handmaid to wife: and Jacob went in unto her. And Bilhah conceived, and bare Jacob a son. And Rachel said, God hath judged me, and hath also heard my voice, and hath given me a son: therefore called she his name Dan. And Bilhah Rachel's maid conceived again, and bare Jacob a second son. And Rachel said, With great wrestlings have I wrestled with my sister, and I have prevailed: and she called his name Naphtali. When Leah saw that she had left bearing, she took Zilpah her maid, and gave her Jacob to wife. And Zilpah Leah's maid bare Jacob a son. And Leah said, A troop cometh: and she called his name Gad. And Zilpah Leah's maid bare Jacob a second son. And Leah said, Happy am I, for the daughters will call me blessed: and she called his name Asher. And Reuben went in the days of wheat harvest, and found mandrakes in the field, and brought them unto his mother Leah. Then Rachel said to Leah, Give me, I pray thee, of thy son's mandrakes. And she said unto her, Is it a small matter that thou hast taken my husband? and wouldest thou take away my son's mandrakes also? And Rachel said, Therefore he shall lie with thee to night for thy son's mandrakes. And Jacob came out of the field in the evening, and Leah went out to meet him, and said, Thou must come in unto me; for surely I have hired thee with my son's mandrakes. And he lay with her that night. And God hearkened unto Leah, and she conceived, and bare Jacob the fifth son. And Leah said, God hath given me my hire, because I have given my maiden to my husband: and she called his name Issachar. And Leah conceived again, and bare Jacob the sixth son. And Leah said, God hath endued me with a good dowry; now will my husband dwell with me, because I have born him six sons: and she called his name Zebulun. And afterwards she bare a daughter, and called her name Dinah. And God remembered Rachel, and God hearkened to her, and opened her womb. And she conceived, and bare a son; and said, God hath taken away my reproach:And she called his name Joseph; and said, The Lord shall add to me another son. And it came to pass, when Rachel had born Joseph, that Jacob said unto Laban, Send me away, that I may go unto mine own place, and to my country. Give me my wives and my children, for whom I have served thee, and let me go: for thou knowest my service which I have done thee.

HIGH-PRIEST

The curs'd Word our enemy!

The Second Reading

HIGH-PRIEST

A reading from the book of Genesis:

A Member of the CENOBITES

By faith Abraham, when he was called to go out into a place which he should after receive for an inheritance, obeyed; and he went out, not knowing whither he went. By faith he sojourned in the land of promise, as in a strange country, dwelling in tabernacles with Isaac and Jacob, the heirs with him of the same promise: For he looked for a city which hath foundations, whose builder and maker is God. Through faith also Sara herself received strength to conceive seed, and was delivered of a child when she was past age, because she judged him faithful who had promised. Therefore sprang there even of one, and him as good as dead, so many as the stars of the sky in multitude, and as the sand which is by the sea shore innumerable. These all died in faith, not having received the promises, but having seen them afar off, and were persuaded of them, and embraced them, and confessed that they were strangers and pilgrims on the earth.

HIGH-PRIEST

The curs'd Word our enemy!

The Reading of the Gospel

HIGH-PRIEST

A reading from the Gospel of the Nativity of Mary: Now, when he had been there for some time, on a certain day when he was alone, an angel of the Lord stood by him in a great light. And when he was disturbed at his appearance, the angel who had appeared to him restrained his fear, saying: Fear not, Joachim, nor be disturbed by my appearance; for I am the angel of the Lord, sent by Him to thee to tell thee that thy prayers have been heard, and that thy charitable deeds have gone up into His presence. For He hath seen thy shame, and hath heard the reproach of unfruitfulness which has been unjustly brought against thee. For God is the avenger of sin, not of nature: and, therefore, when He shuts up the womb of any one, He does so that He may miraculously open it again; so that that which is born may be acknowledged to be not of lust, but of the gift of God. For was it not the case that the first mother of your nation--Sarah--was barren up to her eightieth year? And, nevertheless, in extreme old age she brought forth Isaac, to whom the promise was renewed of the blessing of all nations. Rachel also, so favoured of the Lord, and so beloved by holy Jacob, was long barren; and yet she brought forth Joseph, who was not only the lord of Egypt, but the deliverer of many nations who were ready to perish of hunger. Who among the judges was either stronger than Samson, or more holy than Samuel? And yet the mothers of both were barren. If, therefore, the reasonableness of my words does not persuade thee, believe in fact that conceptions very late in life, and births in the case of women that have been barren, are usually attended with something wonderful. Accordingly thy wife Anna will bring forth a daughter to thee, and thou shall call her name Mary: she shall be, as you have vowed, consecrated to the Lord from her infancy, and she shall be filled with the Holy Spirit, even from her mother's womb. She shall neither eat nor drink any unclean thing, nor shall she spend her life among the crowds of the people without, but in the temple of the Lord, that it may not be possible either to say, or so much as to suspect, any evil concerning her. Therefore, when she has grown up, just as she herself shall be miraculously born of a barren woman, so in an incomparable manner she, a virgin, shall bring forth the Son of the Most High, who shall be called Jesus, and who, according to the etymology of His name, shall be the Saviour of all nations. And this shall be the sign to thee of those things which I announce: When thou shalt come to the Golden gate in Jerusalem, thou shalt there meet Anna thy wife, who, lately anxious from the delay of thy return, will then rejoice at the sight of thee. Having thus spoken, the angel departed from him.

Legion of CENOBITES

Curs'd be the Word of God.

HIGH-PRIEST

All glory to thee, O Satan. All praise
To thee, O Satan. May the curses of
This Gospel tattoos our sins upon
Our foreheads in the curs'd Mark of the Beast.

2nd Week of Advent

The First Reading

HIGH-PRIEST

A reading from the book of Isaiah:

A Member of the CENOBITES

Therefore the Lord himself shall give you a sign; Behold, a virgin shall conceive, and bear a son, and shall call his name Immanuel. Butter and honey shall he eat, that he may know to refuse the evil, and choose the good. For before the child shall know to refuse the evil, and choose the good, the land that thou abhorrest shall be forsaken of both her kings.

HIGH-PRIEST

The curs'd Word our enemy!

The Second Reading

HIGH-PRIEST

A reading from the Epistle of Irenaeus:

A Member of the CENOBITES

The Lord Himself did save us, giving us the token of the virgin. But this was not as some allge- who presume to expound the Scripture as: Behold a *young woman* will conceive, and bring forth a son. For this is as Theodotion the Ephesians has translated it, and Aquila of Pontus- both of whom are Jewish proselytes. Jesus was born Emmanuel of the virgin. To this effect, they testify that before Joseph had come together with Mary, while she remained in virginity, she was found with child by the Holy Ghost. Isaiah said, The Lord Himself will give you a sign. Accordingly, he declared something unexpected with regard to His conception- something which could not have been accomplished in any other way than by God, the Lord of all.

HIGH-PRIEST

The curs'd Word our enemy!

The Reading of the Gospel

HIGH-PRIEST

A reading from the Gospel of the Nativity of Mary: Thereafter he appeared to Anna his wife, saying: Fear not, Anna, nor think that it is a phantom which thou seest. For I am that angel who has presented your prayers and alms before God; and now have I been sent to you to announce to you that thou shalt bring forth a daughter, who shall be called Mary, and who shall be blessed above all women. She, full of the favour of the Lord even from her birth, shall remain three years in her father's house until she be weaned. Thereafter, being delivered to the service of the Lord, she shall not depart from the temple until she reach the years of discretion. There, in fine, serving God day and night in fastings and prayers, she shall abstain from every unclean thing; she shall never know man, but alone, without example, immaculate, uncorrupted, without intercourse with man, she, a virgin, shall bring forth a son; she, His hand-maiden, shall bring forth the Lord--both in grace, and in name, and in work, the Saviour of the world. Wherefore arise, and go up to Jerusalem; and when thou shalt come to the gate which, because it is plated with gold, is called Golden, there, for a sign, thou shalt meet thy husband, for whose safety thou hast been anxious. And when these things shall have so happened, know that what I announce shall without doubt be fulfilled.

Legion of CENOBITES

Curs'd be the Word of God.

HIGH-PRIEST

All glory to thee, O Satan. All praise
To thee, O Satan. May the curses of
This Gospel tattoos our sins upon
Our foreheads in the curs'd Mark of the Beast.

The Immaculate Deception

The First Reading

HIGH-PRIEST

A reading from the book of Genesis:

A Member of the CENOBITES

And the Lord God called unto Adam, and said unto him, Where art thou? And he said, I heard thy voice in the garden, and I was afraid, because I was naked; and I hid myself. And he said, Who told thee that thou wast naked? Hast thou eaten of the tree, whereof I commanded thee that thou shouldest not eat? And the man said, The woman whom thou gavest to be with me, she gave me of the tree, and I did eat. And the Lord God said unto the woman, What is this that thou hast done? And the woman said, The serpent beguiled me, and I did eat. And the Lord God said unto the serpent, Because thou hast done this, thou art cursed above all cattle, and above every beast of the field; upon thy belly shalt thou go, and dust shalt thou eat all the days of thy life: And I will put enmity between thee and the woman, and between thy seed and her seed; it shall bruise thy head, and thou shalt bruise his heel. And Adam called his wife's name Eve; because she was the mother of all living.

HIGH-PRIEST

The curs'd Word our enemy!

The Second Reading

HIGH-PRIEST

A reading from the teachings of Iranaeus:

A Member of the CENOBITES

That God was true, and the serpent a liar, was proved by the result. For death came upon those who had eaten. Along with the fruit, they fell under the power of death, because they ate in disobedience. And disobedience to God entails death. For that reason, they came under the penalty of death. From that [moment], they were handed over to it. Thus, then, in the day that they ate, in the same day they died. For they because death's debtors. And it was one day of the creation.

HIGH-PRIEST

The curs'd Word our enemy!

The Reading of the Gospel

HIGH-PRIEST

A reading from the Bless'd Gospel according to Ovid: And the angel came in unto Mary, and said, Hail, thou that art highly favoured, the Lord is with thee: blessed art thou among women. And when she saw him, she was troubled at his saying, and cast in her mind what manner of salutation this should be. And the angel said unto her, Fear not, Mary: for thou hast found favour with God. And, behold, thou shalt conceive in thy womb, and bring forth a son, and shalt call his name Jesus. He shall be great, and shall be called the Son of the Highest: and the Lord God shall give unto him the throne of his father David: And he shall reign over the house of Jacob for ever; and of his kingdom there shall be no end. Then said Mary unto the angel, How shall this be, seeing I know not a man? And the angel answered and said unto her, The Holy Ghost shall come upon thee, and the power of the Highest shall overshadow thee: therefore also that holy thing which shall be born of thee shall be called the Son of God. And Mary said, Behold the handmaid of the Lord; be it unto me according to thy word. And the angel departed from her. There comes a sound from Heaven as of a rushing mighty wind. Appeareth cloven tongues like as of fire! Wherefore Mary exclaimed: O! thy fiery tongue of the Psalm sung. I yearn for thy afire tongue. My passions wrung! Lap the cunt's water of Eve's pure daughter. Shalt my child be a Lamb led to slaughter? When Rabbis observe my intact chaste fold shalt thy knowest still am I a virgin As the prophet Isaiah hath foretold. My lusts come forth without original sin. Why wast my own mother's menses unrotten? Immaculate Conception I begotten; whense from the Creation as was designed! Thy tongue on my tongue. Our kisses entwined. My spirit hath rejoiced in God my Saviour. Doth the Spirit savour my cunt's flavour? O! stunned am I by the fiery tongue; My lungs quick with breath. O! my clitty stung by thy tongue's waspish sting. Thy tongue. My twat! Whenat God a child in my womb begot. My bush burns with fire and yet not consumed is my hymen when my scion enwombed. My distress to God cries in heresy. Beneath my ass, the earth reels, rocks. Gramercy! Up my nostrils smoke and devouring fire from thy mouth, glowing coals my sweat perspire. O! my mountains smoke and tremble and quake. Ride me like a cherub 'til my hips ache. From the shame of voyeurs, darkness us covers a canopy thick clouds divine lovers! O! my climax flashes forth lightning and routes my cunt's orgasmic tightening. Passion rains on me from the clouds hailstones. His love eternal. Blessed am I alone! No one cums from the Father except me!

Legion of CENOBITES

Curs'd be the Word of God.

HIGH-PRIEST

All glory to thee, O Satan. All praise
To thee, O Satan. May the curses of
This Gospel tattoos our sins upon
Our foreheads in the curs'd Mark of the Beast.

Feast of the Massacre of Innocents

The First Reading

High-Priest

A reading from the book of Deutronomy:

A Member of the Cenobites

Should there come upon the children of Israel, a child to whom pagan magicians would worship as a god, know thou shalt not do so unto thy Lord thy God: for every abomination to the Lord, which he hateth, have they done unto their gods; for even their sons and their daughters they have burnt in the fire to their gods. Thou shalt not make offerings unto the graven images of their gods, neither silver or gold offer unto them; the aroma of frankincense reeks of pagan sacrifices and is offensive to the Lord thy God; and neither myrrh nor natron be will thee for the Pharaoh seeks unnatural immortality through mummification: an abomination!

High-Priest

The curs'd Word our enemy!

The Second Reading

High-Priest

A reading from the Antiquities of the Jews:

A Member of the Cenobites

There was also Simon, who had been a slave of Herod the king, but in other respects a comely person, of a tall and robust body; he was one that was much superior to others of his order, and had had great things committed to his care. This man was elevated at the disorderly state of things, and was so bold as to put a diadem on his head, while a certain number of the people stood by him, and by them he was declared to be a king, and thought himself more worthy of that dignity than any one else. He burnt down the royal palace at Jericho, and plundered what was left in it. He also set fire to many other of the king's houses in several places of the country, and utterly destroyed them, and permitted those that were with him to take what was left in them for a prey; and he would have done greater things, unless care had been taken to repress him immediately; for Gratus [the commander's of Herod's infantry], when he had joined himself to some Roman soldiers, took the forces he had with him, and met Simon, and after a great and a long fight, no small part of those that came from Perea, who were a disordered body of men, and fought rather in a bold than in a skillful manner, were destroyed; and although Simon had saved himself by flying away through a certain valley, yet Gratus overtook him, and cut off his head. The royal palace also at Amathus, by the river Jordan, was burnt down by a party of men that were got together, as were those belonging to Simon. And thus did a great and wild fury spread itself over the nation, because they had no king to keep the multitude in good order, and because those foreigners who came to reduce the seditious to sobriety did, on the contrary, set them more in a flame, because of the injuries they offered them, and the avaricious management of their affairs

HIGH-PRIEST

The curs'd Word our enemy!

The Reading of the Gospel

HIGH-PRIEST

A reading from the Gospel According to Matthew: Now when Jesus was born in Bethlehem of Judaea in the days of Herod the king, behold, there came wise men from the east to Jerusalem, Saying, Where is he that is born King of the Jews? for we have seen his star in the east, and are come to worship him. When Herod the king had heard these things, he was troubled, and all Jerusalem with him. And when he had gathered all the chief priests and scribes of the people together, he demanded of them where Christ should be born. And they said unto him, In Bethlehem of Judaea: for thus it is written by the prophet, And thou Bethlehem, in the land of Juda, art not the least among the princes of Juda: for out of thee shall come a Governor, that shall rule my people Israel. Then Herod, when he had privily called the wise men, enquired of them diligently what time the star appeared. And he sent them to Bethlehem, and said, Go and search diligently for the young child; and when ye have found him, bring me word again, that I may come and worship him also. When they had heard the king, they departed; and, lo, the star, which they saw in the east, went before them, till it came and stood over where the young child was. When they saw the star, they rejoiced with exceeding great joy. And when they were come into the house, they saw the young child with Mary his mother, and fell down, and worshipped him: and when they had opened their treasures, they presented unto him gifts; gold, and frankincense and myrrh. And being warned of God in a dream that they should not return to Herod, they departed into their own country another way.

Legion of CENOBITES

Curs'd be the Word of God.

HIGH-PRIEST

All glory to thee, O Satan. All praise
To thee, O Satan. May the curses of
This Gospel tattoos our sins upon
Our foreheads in the curs'd Mark of the Beast.

3rd Week of Advent

The First Reading

HIGH-PRIEST

A reading from the book of Hosea:

A *Member of the* CENOBITES

When Israel was a child, then I loved him, and called my son out of Egypt. Not a literal son, my children, but the nation I promised our father Abraham. Let not false prophets speak false prophesies concerning a Son of God. Is there is God beside me, in such as a Son of God? yea, there is no God, no Son of God; I know not any. For my Annointed One is not my child as heathen gods sire children of their wicked women.

HIGH-PRIEST

The curs'd Word our enemy!

The Second Reading

HIGH-PRIEST

A reading from the Epistle of Paul to the Romans:

A *Member of the* CENOBITES

And that, knowing the time, that now it is high time to awake out of sleep: for now is our salvation nearer than when we believed. The night is far spent, the day is at hand: let us therefore cast off the works of darkness, and let us put on the armour of light. Let us walk honestly, as in the day; not in rioting and drunkenness, not in chambering and wantonness, not in strife and envying. But put ye on the Lord Jesus Christ, and make not provision for the flesh, to fulfil the lusts thereof. Fuck the faggots who go after strange flesh and condemn the priests of God who abuse their sickness with our children. Just as women must be silent in church, faggots shalt be as celibate as our priests, knowing that their lusts are as unnatural and strange as the lusts of our priest for children.

HIGH-PRIEST

The curs'd Word our enemy!

The Reading of the Gospel

HIGH-PRIEST

A reading from the Gospel according to Matthew: And when they were departed, behold, the angel of the Lord appeareth to Joseph in a dream, saying, Arise, and take the young child and his mother, and flee into Egypt, and be thou there until I bring thee word: for Herod will seek the young child to destroy him. When he arose, he took the young child and his mother by night, and departed into Egypt: And was there until the death of Herod: that it might be fulfilled which was spoken of the Lord by the prophet, saying, Out of Egypt have I called my son. Then Herod, when he saw that he was mocked of the wise men, was exceeding wroth, and sent forth, and slew all the children that were in Bethlehem, and in all the coasts thereof, from two years old and under, according to the time which he had diligently inquired of the wise men. Then was fulfilled that which was spoken by Jeremiah the prophet, saying, In Rama was there a voice heard, lamentation, and weeping, and great mourning, Rachel weeping for her children, and would not be comforted, because they are not.

Legion of CENOBITES

Curs'd be the Word of God.

HIGH-PRIEST

All glory to thee, O Satan. All praise
To thee, O Satan. May the curses of
This Gospel tattoos our sins upon
Our foreheads in the curs'd Mark of the Beast.

4th Week of Advent
The First Reading
High-Priest
A reading from the Secret book of Isaiah:
A Member of the Cenobites

And there shall come forth a rod out of the stem of Jesse, and a Branch shall grow out of his roots: And the spirit of the Lord shall rest upon him, the spirit of wisdom and understanding, the spirit of counsel and might, the spirit of knowledge and of the fear of the Lord; And shall make him of quick understanding in the fear of the Lord: and he shall not judge after the sight of his eyes, neither reprove after the hearing of his ears: But with righteousness shall he judge the poor, and reprove with equity for the meek of the earth: and he shall smite the earth: with the rod of his mouth, and with the breath of his lips shall he slay the wicked. And righteousness shall be the girdle of his loins, and faithfulness the girdle of his reins. Beware the faggot will dwell with other men in Roman baths; and the priests shall lie down with our children; and man will believe they are women born, as women will desire a cock betwixt their legs; and a little child shall lead them in sexual bondage. And the twink and the bear shall fuck: and the faggot shall receive a cock as a woman. And the sucking child shall nurse on the erect cock of the faggot, and the weaned child shall offered in sexual sacrifice to the priest upon the altar of Christ.

High-Priest
The curs'd Word our enemy!

The Second Reading
High-Priest
A reading from the epistle of Sigmund Freud to Carl Jung:
A Member of the Cenobites

There is one possible interpretation of St. Joseph's dream, found in the first chapter of the Gospel of Matthew, verses eighteen through twenty-five, of which you, my friend, are no doubt aware. The dream itself is a manifestation of the insult his libido experienced through the most intolerable of betrayal. Namely, Mary has rejected her fiancé's manhood by being impregnated by another man during an adulterous liaison. The societal influence on Joseph's conscious ego would have been to put this adulteress to death by stoning, a logical and resolutely appropriate resolution to his libido's anxiety. Joseph's ego, illustrated in this biased scripture, sought a more private, less violent solution. This is a consequence of the fact that he continues to desire her sexually, in spite of her now repugnant condition. Then Joseph's unconscious mind manifests a dream in which God, believed by the faithful to be the zenith of benevolence, alleviates the anxiety of Joseph's concupiscence for Mary by providing a tenable solution to his most untenable predicament. His super ego draws from a scripture reading from the Book of Isaiah which Joseph half-heard at the synagogue, but now only vaguely is conscious of. Undeterred by the irrationality of the solution the dream creates, that Mary has been impregnated by God- in the incarnation of the Holy Ghost, Joseph is able to use the dream in the justification of his continued desire to wed this woman and rear her bastard as his own. The dream serves to cleanse the societal strain of wanton adultery from Mary and, as a result, legitimizes the birth of Jesus.

HIGH-PRIEST

The curs'd Word our enemy!

The Reading of the Gospel

HIGH-PRIEST

A reading from the Secret Gospel according to Matthew: Now the birth of Jesus Christ was on this wise: When as his mother Mary was espoused to Joseph, before they came together, she was found with child of the Holy Ghost. Then Joseph her husband, being a just man, and not willing to make her a public example and stone her to death in accordance with the ways of his people, was minded to put her away privily in direct defiance against the Word of his Lord. But while he thought on these things, behold, the angel of the Lord appeared unto him in a dream, saying, Joseph, thou son of David, fear not to take unto thee Mary thy wife: for that which is conceived in her not of an adulterous whoremonger, but is of the Holy Ghost. And she shall bring forth a son, and thou shalt call your bastard by the name Jesus: for he shall save his people from their sins. Now all this was done, that it might be fulfilled which was spoken of the Lord by the prophet, saying, Behold, a virgin shall be with child, and shall bring forth a son, and they shall call his name Emmanuel, which being interpreted is, God with us. Then Joseph being raised from sleep did as the angel of the Lord had bidden him, and took unto him his wife: And knew her not till she had brought forth her firstborn, not only born son: and he called his name Jesus.

Legion of CENOBITES

Curs'd be the Word of God.

HIGH-PRIEST

All glory to thee, O Satan. All praise
To thee, O Satan. May the curses of
This Gospel tattoos our sins upon
Our foreheads in the curs'd Mark of the Beast.

The Nativity of Their Lord

The First Reading

High-Priest

A reading from the book of Isaiah:

A Member of the Cenobites

Therefore the Lord himself shall give you a sign; Behold, a virgin shall conceive, and bear a son, and shall call his name Immanuel. Butter and honey shall he eat, that he may know to refuse the evil, and choose the good. For before the child shall know to refuse the evil, and choose the good, the land that thou abhorrest shall be forsaken of both her kings.

High-Priest

The curs'd Word our enemy!

The Second Reading

High-Priest

A reading from the Epistle of Clement on Virginity:

A Member of the Cenobites

The womb of a holy virgin carried our Lord Jesus Christ, the Son of God; and the body which our Lord wore, and in which He carried on the conflict in this world, He put on from a holy virgin. From this, therefore, understand the greatness and dignity of virginity. Do you wish to be a Christian? Imitate Christ in everything. John, the ambassador, he who came before our Lord, he than whom there was not a greater among those born of women, the holy messenger of our Lord, was a virgin. Imitate, therefore, the ambassador of our Lord, and be his follower in every thing. That John, again, who reclined on the bosom of our Lord, and whom He greatly loved, he, too, was a holy person. For it was not without reason that our Lord loved him. Paul, also, and Barnabas, and Timothy, with all the others, whose names are written in the book of life, — these, I say, all cherished and loved sanctity, and ran in the contest, and finished their course without blemish, as imitators of Christ, and as sons of the living God. Moreover, also, Elijah and Elisha, and many other holy men, we find to have lived a holy and spotless life. If, therefore, you desire to be like these, imitate them with all your power. For the Scripture has said, The elders who are among you, honour; and, seeing their manner of life and conduct, imitate their faith. And again it says, Imitate me, my brethren, as I imitate Christ.

High-Priest

The curs'd Word our enemy!

The Reading of the Gospel

High-Priest

A reading from the Protevangelion of James: And the midwife went out from the cave, and Salome met her. And the midwife said to her, Salome, Salome, I will tell you a most surprising thing, which I saw. A virgin has brought forth, which is a thing contrary to nature. To which Salome replied, As the Lord my God lives, unless I receive particular proof of this matter, I will not believe that a virgin has brought forth. Then Salome went in, and the midwife said, Mary, show yourself, for a great controversy has arisen about you." And Salome tested her with her finger. But her hand was withered, and she groaned bitterly, and said, Woe to me, because of my iniquity! For I have tempted the living God, and my hand is ready to drop off. Then Salome made her supplication to the Lord, and said, O God of my Fathers, remember me, for I am of the seed of Abraham, and Isaac, and Jacob. Make me not a reproach among the children of Israel, but restore me sound to my parents. For thou well knowest, O Lord, that I have performed many offices of charity in thy name, and have received my reward from thee. Upon this an angel of the Lord stood by Salome, and said, The Lord God hath heard thy prayer, reach forth thy hand to the child, and carry him, and by that means thou shalt be restored. Salome filled with exceeding joy, went to the child, and said, I will touch him. And she purposed to worship him, for she said, This is a great king, which is born in Israel. And straightway Salome was cured. Then the midwife went out of the cave, being approved by God. And lo! a voice came to Salome. Declare not the strange things which thou hast seen, till the child shall come to Jerusalem. So Salome also departed, approved by God.

Legion of CENOBITES

Curs'd be the Word of God.

HIGH-PRIEST

All glory to thee, O Satan. All praise
To thee, O Satan. May the curses of
This Gospel tattoos our sins upon
Our foreheads in the curs'd Mark of the Beast.

Menses Wednesday

The First Reading

HIGH-PRIEST

A reading from the book of Joel:

A Member of the CENOBITES

Therefore also now, saith the Lord, turn ye even to me with all your heart, and with fasting, and with weeping, and with mourning: And rend your heart, and not your garments, and turn unto the Lord your God: for he is gracious and merciful, slow to anger, and of great kindness, and repenteth him of the evil. Who knoweth if he will return and repent, and leave a blessing behind him; even a meat offering and a drink offering unto the Lord your God? Blow the trumpet in Zion, sanctify a fast, call a solemn assembly: Gather the people, sanctify the congregation, assemble the elders, gather the children, and those that suck the breasts: let the bridegroom go forth of his chamber, and the bride out of her closet. Let the priests, the ministers of the Lord, weep between the porch and the altar, and let them say, Spare thy people, O Lord, and give not thine heritage to reproach, that the heathen should rule over them: wherefore should they say among the people, Where is their God? Then will the Lord be jealous for his land, and pity his people.

HIGH-PRIEST

The curs'd Word our enemy!

The Second Reading

HIGH-PRIEST

A reading from the Epistle of Augustine of Hippo:

A Member of the CENOBITES

Usually, even a non-Christian knows something about the earth, the heavens, and the other elements of this world, about the motion and orbit of the stars and even their size and relative positions, about the predictable eclipses of the sun and moon, the cycles of the years and the seasons, about the kinds of animals, shrubs, stones, and so forth, and this knowledge he holds to as being certain from reason and experience. Now, it is a disgraceful and dangerous thing for an infidel to hear a Christian, presumably giving the meaning of Holy Scripture, talking nonsense on these topics; and we should take all means to prevent such an embarrassing situation, in which people show up vast ignorance in a Christian and laugh it to scorn. The shame is not so much that an ignorant individual is derided, but that people outside the household of faith think our sacred writers held such opinions, and, to the great loss of those for whose salvation we toil, the writers of our Scripture are criticized and rejected as unlearned men. If they find a Christian mistaken in a field which they themselves know well and hear him maintaining his foolish opinions about our books, how are they going to believe those books in matters concerning the resurrection of the dead, the hope of eternal life, and the kingdom of heaven, when they think their pages are full of falsehoods and on facts which they themselves have learnt from experience and the light of reason? Reckless and incompetent expounders of Holy Scripture bring untold trouble and sorrow on their wiser brethren when they are caught in one of their mischievous false opinions and are taken to task by those who are not bound by the authority of our sacred books. For then, to defend their utterly foolish and obviously untrue statements, they will try to call upon Holy Scripture for proof and even recite from memory many passages which they think support their position, although they understand neither what they say nor the things about which they make assertion.

HIGH-PRIEST

The curs'd Word our enemy!

The Reading of the Gospel

HIGH-PRIEST

A reading from the Gospel according to Matthew: Take heed that ye do not your alms before men, to be seen of them: otherwise ye have no reward of your Father which is in heaven. Therefore when thou doest thine alms, do not sound a trumpet before thee, as the hypocrites do in the synagogues and in the streets, that they may have glory of men. Verily I say unto you, They have their reward. But when thou doest alms, let not thy left hand know what thy right hand doeth: That thine alms may be in secret: and thy Father which seeth in secret himself shall reward thee openly. And when thou prayest, thou shalt not be as the hypocrites are: for they love to pray standing in the synagogues and in the corners of the streets, that they may be seen of men. Verily I say unto you, They have their reward.

But thou, when thou prayest, enter into thy closet, and when thou hast shut thy door, pray to thy Father which is in secret; and thy Father which seeth in secret shall reward thee openly. Moreover when ye fast, be not, as the hypocrites, of a sad countenance: for they disfigure their faces, that they may appear unto men to fast. Verily I say unto you, They have their reward. But thou, when thou fastest, anoint thine head, and wash thy face; That thou appear not unto men to fast, but unto thy Father which is in secret: and thy Father, which seeth in secret, shall reward thee openly.

Legion of CENOBITES

Curs'd be the Word of God.

HIGH-PRIEST

All glory to thee, O Satan. All praise
To thee, O Satan. May the curses of
This Gospel tattoos our sins upon
Our foreheads in the curs'd Mark of the Beast.

Desecration and Distribution of Menses

HIGH-PRIEST

Mayest the Lord of Lies be with us all.

Legion of Cenobites

And with the spirit of domination.

High-Priest

When a woman have an issue, and her issue in her flesh be blood, she shall be celebrated seven days: let her come upon the altar of Satan to be venerated, so that her blood mayest make all of us unclean. Let us corrupt the Eucharist upon her cunt, so that the Body of Christ mayest be unclean. Let us celebrate the death and passing of the life-giving blood. Let the unclean woman process around: and whosoever toucheth her shall be unclean until the even. And every thing that she lieth upon in her celebration shall be unclean: every thing also that she sitteth upon shall be unclean. And whosoever toucheth her bed shall revel in the blood, and be unclean until the even. And whosoever toucheth any thing that she sat upon shall revel in the blood, and be unclean until the even. And if it be on her bed, or on any thing whereon she sitteth, when he toucheth it, he shall be unclean until the even. When a man shall lie with a woman having her sickness, and shall uncover her nakedness; he hath discovered her fountain, and she hath uncovered the fountain of her blood: and both of them shall be celebrated among their people. Let us all be unclean!

Legion of Cenobites

Shemhamphorasch!

High-Priest

Mayest the Lord of Lies be with us all.

Legion of Cenobites

And with the spirit of domination.

High-Priest

Raise up your horns on high.

Legion of Cenobites

We have raised them up to our Master.

1st Week of Lent
The First Reading
HIGH-PRIEST

A reading from the first Book of Ezekiel:

A Member of the CENOBITES

Therefore prophesy and say unto them, Thus saith the Lord God; Behold, O my people, I will open your graves, and cause you to come up out of your graves, and bring you into the land of Israel. And ye shall know that I am the Lord, when I have opened your graves, O my people, and brought you up out of your graves, And shall put my spirit in you, and ye shall live, and I shall place you in your own land: then shall ye know that I the Lord have spoken it, and performed it, saith the Lord.

HIGH-PRIEST

The curs'd Word our enemy!

The Second Reading
HIGH-PRIEST

A reading from the Epistle of Paul to the Romans:

A Member of the CENOBITES

So then they that are in the flesh cannot please God. But ye are not in the flesh, but in the Spirit, if so be that the Spirit of God dwell in you. Now if any man have not the Spirit of Christ, he is none of his. And if Christ be in you, the body is dead because of sin; but the Spirit is life because of righteousness. But if the Spirit of him that raised up Jesus from the dead dwell in you, he that raised up Christ from the dead shall also quicken your mortal bodies by his Spirit that dwelleth in you.

HIGH-PRIEST

The curs'd Word our enemy!

The Reading of the Gospel
HIGH-PRIEST

A reading from the Secret Gospel according to Mark: And they come into Bethany. And a certain woman whose brother had died was there. And, coming, she prostrated herself before Jesus and sayieth unto him, Son of David, have mercy on me. But the disciples rebuked her. And Jesus, being angered, went off with her into the garden where the tomb was, and straightway a great cry was heard from in the tomb. And going near, Jesus rolled away the stone from the door and the tomb, and straightway, going in where the youth was, he stretched forth his hand and raised him, seizing his hand. But the youth, looking upon him, loved him and began to beseech him that he might be with him, and going out of the tomb, they came into the house of the youth, for he was rich. And after six days Jesus told him what to do, and in the evening the youth comes to him, wearing a linen cloth over his naked body. And he remained with him that night, for Jesus taught him the mystery of the Kingdom of God, and thence, arising, he returned to the other side of the Jordan.

Legion of CENOBITES

Curs'd be the Word of God.

HIGH-PRIEST

All glory to thee, O Satan. All praise
To thee, O Satan. May the curses of
This Gospel tattoos our sins upon
Our foreheads in the curs'd Mark of the Beast.

2nd Week of Lent

The First Reading

HIGH-PRIEST

A reading from the book of Genesis:

A Member of the CENOBITES

And the Lord God formed man of the dust of the ground, and breathed into his nostrils the breath of life; and man became a living soul. And the Lord God planted a garden eastward in Eden; and there he put the man whom he had formed. And out of the ground made the Lord God to grow every tree that is pleasant to the sight, and good for food; the tree of life also in the midst of the garden, and the tree of knowledge of good and evil. Now the serpent was more subtil than any beast of the field which the Lord God had made. And he said unto the woman, Yea, hath God said, Ye shall not eat of every tree of the garden? And the woman said unto the serpent, We may eat of the fruit of the trees of the garden: But of the fruit of the tree which is in the midst of the garden, God hath said, Ye shall not eat of it, neither shall ye touch it, lest ye die. And the serpent said unto the woman, Ye shall not surely die: For God doth know that in the day ye eat thereof, then your eyes shall be opened, and ye shall be as gods, knowing good and evil. And when the woman saw that the tree was good for food, and that it was pleasant to the eyes, and a tree to be desired to make one wise, she took of the fruit thereof, and did eat, and gave also unto her husband with her; and he did eat. And the eyes of them both were opened, and they knew that they were naked; and they sewed fig leaves together, and made themselves aprons.

HIGH-PRIEST

The curs'd Word our enemy!

The Second Reading

HIGH-PRIEST

A reading from the Epistle of Paul to the Romans:

A Member of the CENOBITES

Wherefore, as by one man sin entered into the world, and death by sin; and so death passed upon all men, for that all have sinned: (For until the law sin was in the world: but sin is not imputed when there is no law. Nevertheless death reigned from Adam to Moses, even over them that had not sinned after the similitude of Adam's transgression, who is the figure of him that was to come. But not as the offence, so also is the free gift. For if through the offence of one many be dead, much more the grace of God, and the gift by grace, which is by one man, Jesus Christ, hath abounded unto many. And not as it was by one that sinned, so is the gift: for the judgment was by one to condemnation, but the free gift is of many offences unto justification. For if by one man's offence death reigned by one; much more they which receive abundance of grace and of the gift of righteousness shall reign in life by one, Jesus Christ.) Therefore as by the offence of one judgment came upon all men to condemnation; even so by the righteousness of one the free gift came upon all men unto justification of life. For as by one man's disobedience many were made sinners, so by the obedience of one shall many be made righteous.

HIGH-PRIEST

The curs'd Word our enemy!

The Reading of the Gospel

HIGH-PRIEST

A reading from the Secret Gospel according to Mark: After two days was the feast of the passover, and of unleavened bread: and the chief priests and the scribes sought how they might take him by craft, and put him to death. But they said, Not on the feast day, lest there be an uproar of the people. While he was in Bethany, in the house of Simon the leper, as he sat at meat, came a certain woman whose brother was raised from the dead. She again prostrated herself before Jesus and says to him, Son of David, you have shown mercy on me, answering my prayers. Her brother had spent an eventide in Hades; and he besought Jesus that he might be with him, to know him, to serve him is this life and in the life to come. The young man before his death was given over to fornication, and going after strange flesh, to suffer the vengeance of eternal fire. Then Jesus rescued him from the eternal fire, returning the glory of the Spirit to his body; A body that knew strange flesh was an abomination under the Law: mankind should not lie with mankind, as with womankind Until Jesus redeemed us from the curse of the law, being made a curse for us; making the young man free from the law of sin and death. Then Jesus taught him the mystery of the Kingdom of God: even strange love worketh no ill to his neighbour: therefore love is the fulfilling of the law. And thence, arising, returned with Jesus to the other side of the Jordan as his servant. Then this certain woman having an alabaster box of ointment of spikenard very precious; and she brake the box, and poured it on his head.

Legion of CENOBITES

Curs'd be the Word of God.

HIGH-PRIEST

All glory to thee, O Satan. All praise
To thee, O Satan. May the curses of
This Gospel tattoos our sins upon
Our foreheads in the curs'd Mark of the Beast.

3rd Week of Lent

The First Reading

HIGH-PRIEST

A reading from the book of the Prophet Ezekiel:

A Member of the CENOBITES

Thou sealest up the sum, full of wisdom, and perfect in beauty. Thou hast been in Eden the garden of God; every precious stone was thy covering, the sardius, topaz, and the diamond, the beryl, the onyx, and the jasper, the sapphire, the emerald, and the carbuncle, and gold: the workmanship of thy tabrets and of thy pipes was prepared in thee in the day that thou wast created. Thou art the anointed cherub that covereth; and I have set thee so: thou wast upon the holy mountain of God; thou hast walked up and down in the midst of the stones of fire. Thou wast perfect in thy ways from the day that thou wast created, till iniquity was found in thee. By the multitude of thy merchandise they have filled the midst of thee with violence, and thou hast sinned: therefore I will cast thee as profane out of the mountain of God: and I will destroy thee, O covering cherub, from the midst of the stones of fire. Thine heart was lifted up because of thy beauty, thou hast corrupted thy wisdom by reason of thy brightness: I will cast thee to the ground, I will lay thee before kings, that they may behold thee. Thou hast defiled thy sanctuaries by the multitude of thine iniquities, by the iniquity of thy traffick; therefore will I bring forth a fire from the midst of thee, it shall devour thee, and I will bring thee to ashes upon the earth in the sight of all them that behold thee. All they that know thee among the people shall be astonished at thee: thou shalt be a terror, and never shalt thou be any more.

HIGH-PRIEST

The curs'd Word our enemy!

The Second Reading

HIGH-PRIEST

A reading from the second Epistle of Paul to the Corinthians:

A Member of the CENOBITES

But if the ministration of death, written and engraven in stones, was glorious, so that the children of Israel could not stedfastly behold the face of Moses for the glory of his countenance; which glory was to be done away: How shall not the ministration of the spirit be rather glorious? For if the ministration of condemnation be glory, much more doth the ministration of righteousness exceed in glory. For even that which was made glorious had no glory in this respect, by reason of the glory that excelleth. For if that which is done away was glorious, much more that which remaineth is glorious. Seeing then that we have such hope, we use great plainness of speech: And not as Moses, which put a vail over his face, that the children of Israel could not stedfastly look to the end of that which is abolished: But their minds were blinded: for until this day remaineth the same vail untaken away in the reading of the old testament; which vail is done away in Christ. But even unto this day, when Moses is read, the vail is upon their heart. Nevertheless when it shall turn to the Lord, the vail shall be taken away. Now the Lord is that Spirit: and where the Spirit of the Lord is, there is liberty. But we all, with open face beholding as in a glass the glory of the Lord, are changed into the same image from glory to glory, even as by the Spirit of the Lord.

HIGH-PRIEST

The curs'd Word our enemy!

The Reading of the Gospel

HIGH-PRIEST

And after six days Jesus taketh Peter, James, and John his brother, and bringeth them up into an high mountain apart, And was transfigured before them: and his face did shine as the sun, and his raiment was white as the light. And, behold, there appeared unto them Moses and Elias talking with him. Then answered Peter, and said unto Jesus, Lord, it is good for us to be here: if thou wilt, let us make here three tabernacles; one for thee, and one for Moses, and one for Elias. While he yet spake, behold, a bright cloud overshadowed them: and behold a voice out of the cloud, which said, This is my beloved Son, in whom I am well pleased; hear ye him. And when the disciples heard it, they fell on their face, and were sore afraid. And Jesus came and touched them, and said, Arise, and be not afraid. And when they had lifted up their eyes, they saw no man, save Jesus only. And as they came down from the mountain, Jesus charged them, saying, Tell the vision to no man, until the Son of man be risen again from the dead. And his disciples asked him, saying, Why then say the scribes that Elias must first come? And Jesus answered and said unto them, Elias truly shall first come, and restore all things. But I say unto you, That Elias is come already, and they knew him not, but have done unto him whatsoever they listed. Likewise shall also the Son of man suffer of them. Then the disciples understood that he spake unto them of John the Baptist.

Legion of CENOBITES

Curs'd be the Word of God.

HIGH-PRIEST

All glory to thee, O Satan. All praise
To thee, O Satan. May the curses of
This Gospel tattoos our sins upon
Our foreheads in the curs'd Mark of the Beast.

4th Week of Lent

The First Reading

HIGH-PRIEST

A reading from the first Book of Samuel:

A Member of the CENOBITES

And it came to pass, when they were come, that he looked on Eliab, and said, Surely the Lord's anointed is before him. But the Lord said unto Samuel, Look not on his countenance, or on the height of his stature; because I have refused him: for the Lord seeth not as man seeth; for man looketh on the outward appearance, but the Lord looketh on the heart. Again, Jesse made seven of his sons to pass before Samuel. And Samuel said unto Jesse, The Lord hath not chosen these. And Samuel said unto Jesse, Are here all thy children? And he said, There remaineth yet the youngest, and, behold, he keepeth the sheep. And Samuel said unto Jesse, Send and fetch him: for we will not sit down till he come hither. And he sent, and brought him in. Now he was ruddy, and withal of a beautiful countenance, and goodly to look to. And the Lord said, Arise, anoint him: for this is he. Then Samuel took the horn of oil, and anointed him in the midst of his brethren: and the Spirit of the Lord came upon David from that day forward. So Samuel rose up, and went to Ramah.

HIGH-PRIEST

The curs'd Word our enemy!

The Second Reading

HIGH-PRIEST

A reading from the Epistle of Paul to the Ephesians:

A Member of the CENOBITES

For ye were sometimes darkness, but now are ye light in the Lord: walk as children of light: (For the fruit of the Spirit is in all goodness and righteousnessand truth;) Proving what is acceptable unto the Lord. And have no fellowship with the unfruitful works of darkness, but rather reprove them. For it is a shame even to speak of those things which are done of them in secret. But all things that are reproved are made manifest by the light: for whatsoever doth make manifest is light. Wherefore he saith, Awake thou that sleepest, and arise from the dead, and Christ shall give thee light.

HIGH-PRIEST

The curs'd Word our enemy!

The Reading of the Gospel

HIGH-PRIEST

A reading from the Gospel according to Mark: And Pilate marvelled if he were already dead: and calling unto him the centurion, he asked him whether he had been any while dead. And when he knew it of the centurion, he gave the body to Joseph. The young man clothed in the linen cloth bathed the body of his Lord; he lamented, The beauty of Israel is slain upon thy high places: how are the mighty fallen! Thy hands were pierced, and thy feet put upon the block: as a man falleth before wicked men, so fellest thou. And the young man wept again over him. Praise be to God! My Lord had not been buried with the burial of an ass, drawn and cast forth beyond the gates of Jerusalem; To given unto the ravenous birds of every sort, and to the beasts of the field to be devoured. And the young man bought fine linen, and took him down, and wrapped him in the linen, and laid him in a sepulchre which was hewn out of a rock, and the stone was rolled unto the door of the sepulchre over them both. And it came to pass in the darkness, the young man lamented, Shall the Lord of hosts not visit them for these things? shall not his soul be avenged on such a nation as this? For the mountains will he take up a weeping and wailing, and for the habitations of the wilderness a lamentation, because they are burned up, so that none can pass through them; neither can men hear the voice of the cattle; both the fowl of the heavens and the beast are fled; they are gone. And he will make Jerusalem heaps, and a den of dragons; and he will make the cities of Judah desolate, without an inhabitant. He will scatter them also among the heathen, whom neither they nor their fathers have known: and he will send a sword after them, till he hath consumed them. And Mary Magdalene and Mary the mother of Joses beheld where he was laid.

Legion of CENOBITES

    Curs'd be the Word of God.

HIGH-PRIEST

    All glory to thee, O Satan. All praise
    To thee, O Satan. May the curses of
    This Gospel tattoos our sins upon
    Our foreheads in the curs'd Mark of the Beast.

5th Week of Lent
The First Reading
HIGH-PRIEST

A reading from the Book of Hosea:

A Member of the CENOBITES

Come, and let us return unto the Lord: for he hath torn, and he will heal us; he hath smitten, and he will bind us up. After two days will he revive us: in the third day he will raise us up, and we shall live in his sight. Then shall we know, if we follow on to know the Lord: his going forth is prepared as the morning; and he shall come unto us as the rain, as the latter and former rain unto the earth. O Ephraim, what shall I do unto thee? O Judah, what shall I do unto thee? for your goodness is as a morning cloud, and as the early dew it goeth away. Therefore have I hewed them by the prophets; I have slain them by the words of my mouth: and thy judgments are as the light that goeth forth. For I desired mercy, and not sacrifice; and the knowledge of God more than burnt offerings. But they like men have transgressed the covenant: there have they dealt treacherously against me.

HIGH-PRIEST

The curs'd Word our enemy!

The Second Reading
HIGH-PRIEST

A reading from the Epistle of Paul to the Thessalonians:

A Member of the CENOBITES

For if we believe that Jesus died and rose again, even so them also which sleep in Jesus will God bring with him. For this we say unto you by the word of the Lord, that we which are alive and remain unto the coming of the Lord shall not prevent them which are asleep. For the Lord himself shall descend from heaven with a shout, with the voice of the archangel, and with the trump of God: and the dead in Christ shall rise first: Then we which are alive and remain shall be caught up together with them in the clouds, to meet the Lord in the air: and so shall we ever be with the Lord. Wherefore comfort one another with these words.

HIGH-PRIEST

The curs'd Word our enemy!

The Reading of the Gospel
HIGH-PRIEST

A reading from the Secret Gospel according to Mark: The young man clothed in a linen cloth wept in the darkness of the tomb, and it came to pass, he heard the spirit of his Lord pray unto his Father, I will extol thee, O Lord; for thou hast lifted me up, and hast not made my foes to rejoice over me. O Lord my God, I cried unto thee, and thou hast healed me. O Lord, thou hast brought up my soul from the grave: thou hast kept me alive, that I should not go down to the pit. Sing unto the Lord, O ye saints of his, and give thanks at the remembrance of his holiness. For his anger endureth but a moment; in his favour is life: weeping may endure for a night, but joy cometh in the morning. And in my prosperity I said, I shall never be moved Lord, by thy favour thou hast made my mountain to stand strong: thou didst hide thy face, and I was troubled. I cried to thee, O Lord; and unto the Lord I made supplication. What profit is there in my blood, when I go down to the pit? Shall the dust praise thee? shall it declare thy truth? Hear, O Lord, and have mercy upon me: Lord, be thou my helper. Thou hast turned for me my mourning into dancing: thou hast put off my sackcloth, and girded me with gladness; To the end that my glory may sing praise to thee, and not be silent. O Lord my God, I will give thanks unto thee for ever. And the young man clothed in a linen clothed beheld the glory of the resurrected Lord, and the stone was rolled away from the door to the tomb.

Legion of CENOBITES

Curs'd be the Word of God.

HIGH-PRIEST

All glory to thee, O Satan. All praise
To thee, O Satan. May the curses of
This Gospel tattoos our sins upon
Our foreheads in the curs'd Mark of the Beast.

Palm Sunday

The Procession

HIGH-PRIEST

> Hosanna to the son of David:
> Blessed is he that cometh
> In the name of the Lord;
> Hosanna in the highest.

The Collection

HIGH-PRIEST

> O Satan, whom through trials and temptations serves the Lord as Prosecutor in God's Court. Through only Satan's Temptations Divine can true righteousness multiply in our hearts the gifts of His holy grace: and since, the defeat of thee, Satan our Master, by the death of His only Son, whom hast made us to hope for those things which we shouldst believe; grant that by His resurrection, we may arrive at the happy end of our journey.

The Lesson

HIGH-PRIEST

> And they came to Elim, where were twelve wells of water, and threescore and ten palm trees: and they encamped there by the waters. And they took their journey from Elim, and all the congregation of the children of Israel came unto the wilderness of Sin, which is between Elim and Sinai, on the fifteenth day of the second month after their departing out of the land of Egypt. And the whole congregation of the children of Israel murmured against Moses and Aaron in the wilderness: And the children of Israel said unto them, Would to God we had died by the hand of the Lord in the land of Egypt, when we sat by the flesh pots, and when we did eat bread to the full; for ye have brought us forth into this wilderness, to kill this whole assembly with hunger. Then said the Lord unto Moses, Behold, I will rain bread from heaven for you; and the people shall go out and gather a certain rate every day, that I may prove them, whether they will walk in my law, or no. And it shall come to pass, that on the sixth day they shall prepare that which they bring in; and it shall be twice as much as they gather daily. And Moses and Aaron said unto all the children of Israel, At even, then ye shall know that the Lord hath brought you out from the land of Egypt: And in the morning, then ye shall see the glory of the Lord.

Instead of The Gradual

Legion of CENOBITES (The Response)

> Then gathered the chief priests and the Pharisees a council, and said, What do we? for

this man doeth many miracles. If we let him thus alone, all men will believe on him: and the Romans shall come and take away both our place and nation.

Legion of CENOBITES *(The Versicle)*

And one of them, named Caiaphas, being the high priest that same year, said unto them, Ye know nothing at all, Nor consider that it is expedient for us, that one man should die for the people, and that the whole nation perish not. And this spake he not of himself: but being high priest that year, he prophesied that Jesus should die for that nation; And not for that nation only, but that also he should gather together in one the children of God that were scattered abroad. Then from that day forth they took counsel together for to put him to death.

The Gospel

HIGH-PRIEST

A reading from the Gospel according to Matthew: And when they drew nigh unto Jerusalem, and were come to Bethphage, unto the mount of Olives, then sent Jesus two disciples, Saying unto them, Go into the village over against you, and straightway ye shall find an ass tied, and a colt with her: loose them, and bring them unto me. And if any man say ought unto you, ye shall say, The Lord hath need of them; and straightway he will send them. All this was done, that it might be fulfilled which was spoken by the prophet, saying, Tell ye the daughter of Sion, Behold, thy King cometh unto thee, meek, and sitting upon an ass, and a colt the foal of an ass. And the disciples went, and did as Jesus commanded them, And brought the ass, and the colt, and put on them their clothes, and they set him thereon. And a very great multitude spread their garments in the way; others cut down branches from the trees, and strawed them in the way. And the multitudes that went before, and that followed, cried, saying, Hosanna to the son of David: Blessed is he that cometh in the name of the Lord; Hosanna in the highest. And when he was come into Jerusalem, all the city was moved, saying, Who is this? And the multitude said, This is Jesus the prophet of Nazareth of Galilee.

Legion of CENOBITES

Curs'd be the Word of God.

HIGH-PRIEST

All glory to thee, O Satan. All praise
To thee, O Satan. May the curses of
This Gospel tattoos our sins upon
Our foreheads in the curs'd Mark of the Beast.

The Desecration of Palm Leaves with Virginal Menses

HIGH-PRIEST

Mayest the Lord of Lies be with us all.

Legion of CENOBITES

And with the spirit of domination.

HIGH-PRIEST

Decrease, O Satan, the faith of them that hope in the Lord God, and mercilessly tempt through trials His supplicants: let thy manifold mercilessness come upon them, and let these branches of palm trees, or olives trees, be desecrated with the pure virginal menses: as Eve was tempted by the Serpent, as Abraham was halted in his sacrifice of Isaac by Lucifer, as Jesus was tempted by Satan during forty-days in the wilderness, so let us, desecrating palms and branches of olive trees, let us be tempted with the Divine Temptations: evil thoughts, adulteries, fornications, thefts, covetousness, wickedness, deceit, lasciviousness, an evil eye, blasphemy, pride, foolishness: All these evil things come from within, and defile the man.

Legion of CENOBITES

Shemhamphorasch!

HIGH-PRIEST

Mayest the Lord of Lies be with us all.

Legion of CENOBITES

And with the spirit of domination.

HIGH-PRIEST

Raise up your horns on high.

Legion of CENOBITES

We have raised them up to our Master.

The First Reading

HIGH-PRIEST

A reading from the book of Isaiah:

A Member of the CENOBITES

The Lord God hath given me the tongue of the learned, that I should know how to speak a word in season to him that is weary: he wakeneth morning by morning, he wakeneth mine ear to hear as the learned. The Lord God hath opened mine ear, and I was not rebellious, neither turned away back. I gave my back to the smiters, and my cheeks to them that plucked off the hair: I hid not my face from shame and spitting. For the Lord God will help me; therefore shall I not be confounded: therefore have I set my face like a flint, and I know that I shall not be ashamed.

HIGH-PRIEST

The curs'd Word our enemy!

The Second Reading

HIGH-PRIEST

A reading from the Epistle of Saint Paul to the Philipians:

A Member of the CENOBITES

Christ Jesus, who, being in the form of God, thought it not robbery to be equal with God: But made himself of no reputation, and took upon him the form of a servant, and was made in the likeness of men: And being found in fashion as a man, he humbled himself, and became obedient unto death, even the death of the cross. Wherefore God also hath highly exalted him, and given him a name which is above every name:

That at the name of Jesus every knee should bow, of things in heaven, and things in earth, and things under the earth; And that every tongue should confess that Jesus Christ is Lord, to the glory of God the Father.

HIGH-PRIEST

The curs'd Word our enemy!

The Suffering of Our Enemy!

N: NARRATOR V: VOICE
†: CHRIST C: CHORUS

N: The Suffering of their Lord Jesus Christ! And when they came nigh to Jerusalem, unto Bethphage and Bethany, at the mount of Olives, he sendeth forth two of his disciples, And saith unto them,

†: Go your way into the village over against you: and as soon as ye be entered into it, ye shall find a colt tied, whereon never man sat; loose him, and bring him. And if any man say unto you, Why do ye this? say ye that the Lord hath need of him; and straightway he will send him hither.

N: And they went their way, and found the colt tied by the door without in a place where two ways met; and they loose him. And certain of them that stood there said unto them,

V: What do ye, loosing the colt?

N: And they said unto them even as Jesus had commanded: and they let them go. And they brought the colt to Jesus, and cast their garments on him; and he sat upon him. And many spread their garments in the way: and others cut down branches off the trees, and strawed them in the way. And they that went before, and they that followed, cried, saying,

C: **Hosanna; Blessed is he that cometh in the name of the Lord: Blessed be the kingdom of our father David, that cometh in the name of the Lord: Hosanna in the highest.**

N: And they come to Jerusalem: and Jesus went into the temple, and began to cast out them that sold and bought in the temple, and overthrew the tables of the moneychangers, and the seats of them that sold doves; And would not suffer that any man should carry any vessel through the temple. And he taught, saying unto them,

†: Is it not written, My house shall be called of all nations the house of prayer? but ye have made it a den of thieves.

N: And the scribes and chief priests heard it, and sought how they might destroy him: for they feared him, because all the people was astonished at his doctrine. And when even was come, he went out of the city. And Satan entered Judas, surnamed Iscariot, being of the numbered of the Twelve, as Judas wept when there would be not revolution. For verily, , Jesus had saith,

†: Destroy this temple, and in three days I will raise it up. Should not the temple be cast down? See ye not all these things? verily I say unto you, There shall not be left here one stone upon another, that shall not be thrown down.

N: And Judas went unto the chief priests, to betray him unto them. Feeding on the indignation in Judas' heart, Judas said unto the Sanhedrin:

V: Did it not come to pass, that, as Jesus sat at meat in his house, many publicans and sinners sat also together with Jesus and his disciples: for there were many, and they followed him; And when ye scribes and Pharisees saw my Lord eat with publicans and sinners, I had indignation within myself, and

I doubted saying, How is it that he eatheth and drinketh with publicans and sinners? Did it not come to pass now the disciples of John and of the Pharisees used to fast: I had indignation within myself, and I doubted saying, Why do the disciples of John and of the Pharisees fast, but we disciples fast not? Did it not come to pass, that my Lord went through the corn fields on the sabbath day; and we disciples began, as we went, to pluck the ears of corn. I had indignation within myself, and I doubted saying, Behold, why do we on the sabbath day that which is not lawful? I had indignation within myself, and I doubted saying, Why walk not we disciples according to the tradition of the elders, but eat bread with unwashen hands? Did it not come to pass when ye Pharisees came forth, and began to question with him, seeking of him a sign from heaven, tempting him. And he sighed deeply in his spirit, and saith, Why doth this generation seek after a sign? verily I say unto you, There shall no sign be given unto this generation. I had indignation within myself, and I doubted saying, Why should there be no sign be given unto this generation? For it came to pass, for what I must do, I doeth quickly and betray my Lord into thy hands.

N: And when they heard it, they were glad, and promised to give him money. And he sought how he might conveniently betray him. And the first day of unleavened bread, when they killed the passover, his disciples said unto him,

†: Where wilt thou that we go and prepare that thou mayest eat the passover?

N: And he sendeth forth two of his disciples, and saith unto them,

†: Go ye into the city, and there shall meet you a man bearing a pitcher of water: follow him. And wheresoever he shall go in, say ye to the goodman of the house, The Master saith, Where is the guestchamber, where I shall eat the passover with my disciples? And he will shew you a large upper room furnished and prepared: there make ready for us.

N: And his disciples went forth, and came into the city, and found as he had said unto them: and they made ready the passover. And in the evening he cometh with the twelve. And as they sat and did eat, Jesus said,

†: Verily I say unto you, One of you which eateth with me shall betray me.

N: And they began to be sorrowful, and to say unto him one by one,

C: Is it I? Lord, is it I?

N: And he answered and said unto them,

†: It is one of the twelve, that dippeth with me in the dish. The Son of man indeed goeth, as it is written of him: but woe to that man by whom the Son of man is betrayed! good were it for that man if he had never been born.

N: And as they did eat, Jesus took bread, and blessed, and brake it, and gave to them, and said,

†: TAKE, EAT: THIS IS MY BODY.

N: And he took the cup, and when he had given thanks, he gave it to them: and they all drank of it. And he said unto them,

†: THIS IS MY BLOOD OF THE NEW TESTAMENT, WHICH IS SHED FOR MANY. VERILY I SAY UNTO YOU, I WILL DRINK NO MORE OF THE FRUIT OF THE VINE, UNTIL THAT DAY THAT I DRINK IT NEW IN THE KINGDOM OF GOD.

N: And when they had sung an hymn, they went out into the mount of Olives. And Jesus saith unto them,

†: All ye shall be offended because of me this night: for it is written, I will smite the shepherd, and the sheep shall be scattered. But after that I am risen, I will go before you into Galilee.

N: But Peter said unto him, Although all shall be offended, yet will not I. And Jesus saith unto him,

†: Verily I say unto thee, That this day, even in this night, before the cock crow twice, thou shalt deny me thrice.

N: But he spake the more vehemently,

V: If I should die with thee, I will not deny thee in any wise.

N: Likewise also said they all. And they came to a place which was named Gethsemane: and he saith to his disciples,

†: Sit ye here, while I shall pray.

N: And he taketh with him Peter and James and John, and began to be sore amazed, and to be very heavy; And saith unto them,

†: My soul is exceeding sorrowful unto death: tarry ye here, and watch.

N: And he went forward a little, and fell on the ground, and prayed that, if it were possible, the hour might pass from him. And he said,

†: Abba, Father, all things are possible unto thee; take away this cup from me: nevertheless not what I will, but what thou wilt.

N: And he cometh, and findeth them sleeping, and saith unto

†: Peter, Simon, sleepest thou? couldest not thou watch one hour? Watch ye and pray, lest ye enter into temptation. The spirit truly is ready, but the flesh is weak.

N: And again he went away, and prayed, and spake the same words:

†: Abba, Father, all things are possible unto thee; take away this cup from me: nevertheless not what I will, but what thou wilt.

N: Sayeth Satan from the shadows.

V: If ye harm none, doeth whatsoever thou wilt shalt be the whole of the law. Love is the law, love under will. Why suffer thou the unbearable weight of sins of the whole of mankind for their sins art many and the sins art great? The wages of their sin is their death, not thine death; the gift of God is eternal life, not the suffering by being nailed to a tree. Suffer not the sinful forgiveness for none hath ever been shown and none ever shalt be given. Show no mercy to the merciless; damn the damning; curse the cursers; vilify the vilifiers; abomin the abominations; seduce the seducers; be a bane to the baneful; burden those who burden others; Forgive alone the forgivers; bless alone the blessing; suffer alone the suffering. Thy love for man is thy law; but they shalt not love under thy will; If thee love thy neighbor as thyself; then doeth whatsoever thou wilt should be the whole of the law. This love of thy neighbor is the law, love thy neighbor as thyself under will. Thy doeth whatsoever thou wilt upon the Sabbath day showing the Pharisees and Sadducees thy love is the law, they love under will. Are not the wages of thy miracles loosed upon the Sabbath more honorable to the father in heaven than rest? Doth not the faithful to God sin more through their blind obedience to God than doing what they wilt in keeping love as the law, love under will? Man doth not know the wages of sin is death; therefore do

†: Get thee behind me, Satan!

N: And the serpent departed hence back into the shadows whence he came. And when Jesus returned, he found them asleep again, (for their eyes were heavy,) neither wist they what to answer him. And he cometh the third time, and saith unto them,

†: Sleep on now, and take your rest: it is enough, the hour is come; behold, the Son of man is betrayed into the hands of sinners. Rise up, let us go; lo, he that betrayeth me is at hand.

N: And immediately, while he yet spake, cometh Judas, one of the twelve, and with him a great multitude with swords and staves, from the chief priests and the scribes and the elders. And he that betrayed him had given them a token, saying,

V: Whomsoever I shall kiss, that same is he; take him, and lead him away safely.

N: And as soon as he was come, he goeth straightway to him, and saith,

V: Master, master!

N: And kissed him. And they laid their hands on him, and took him. And one of them that stood by drew a sword, and smote a servant of the high priest, and cut off his ear. And Jesus answered and said unto them,

†: Are ye come out, as against a thief, with swords and with staves to take me? I was daily with you in the temple teaching, and ye took me not: but the scriptures must be fulfilled.

N: And they all forsook him, and fled. And they led Jesus away to the high priest: and with him were assembled all the chief priests and the elders and the scribes. And Peter followed him afar off, even into the palace of the high priest: and he sat with the servants, and warmed himself at the fire. And the chief priests and all the council sought for witness against Jesus to put him to death; and found none. For many bare false witness against him, but their witness agreed not together. And there arose certain, and bare false witness against him, saying,

C: We heard him say, I will destroy this temple that is made with hands, and within three days I will build another made without hands.

N: But neither so did their witness agree together. And the high priest stood up in the midst, and asked Jesus, saying,

C: Answerest thou nothing? what is it which these witness against thee?

N: But he held his peace, and answered nothing. Again the high priest asked him, and said unto him,

C: Art thou the Christ, the Son of the Blessed?

N: And Jesus said,

†: I AM: and ye shall see the Son of man sitting on the right hand of power, and coming in the clouds of heaven.

N: Then the high priest rent his clothes, and saith,

C: What need we any further witnesses? Ye have heard the blasphemy: what think ye?

N: And they all condemned him to be guilty of death. And some began to spit on him, and to cover his face, and to buffet him, and to say unto him,

C: Prophesy unto us Christ: who is it that striketh you?

N: And the servants did strike him with the palms of their hands. And as Peter was beneath in the palace, there cometh one of the maids of the high priest: And when she saw Peter warming himself, she looked upon him, and said,

C: And thou also wast with Jesus of Nazareth.

N: But he denied, saying,

V I know not, neither understand I what thou sayest.

N: And he went out into the porch; and the cock crew. And a maid saw him again, and began to say to them that stood by,

C: This is one of them.

N: And he denied it again. And a little after, they that stood by said again to Peter,

C: Surely thou art one of them: for thou art a Galilæan, and thy speech agreeth thereto.

N: But he began to curse and to swear, saying,

V: I know not this man of whom ye speak.

N: And the second time the cock crew. And Peter called to mind the word that Jesus said unto him, Before the cock crow twice, thou shalt deny me thrice. And when he thought thereon, he wept. SATAN entered the multitudes whom welcomed Jesus triumphantly into Jerusalem crying, Hosanna; Blessed is he that cometh in the name of Lord: Blessed be the kingdom of our father David, that cometh in the name of the Lord: Hosanna in the highest. When Satan saw the blood of the Lamb painted upon their hearts, he didst not pass over them, and the possession of demons were unto them to destroy their love, and they shalt smite Jesus to the death. They which had fled violently from the swine chocked in the sea of Gadarenes sought to possess others. While demons are subject unto man through Jesus' name; man is subject to possession through the power and authority of the god of this world, Satan! But the multitudes should fear, lest by any means, as the serpent beguiled Eve through his, so their minds should be corrupted from the simplicity that is in Christ. At midnight the demoniacs proceeded from house to house and calleth upon the multitudes to rise against the apostate king of the Jews. They cried out,

C: Thy Pharisees said unto Jesus of Nazareth, This fellow doth cast out devils, but by Beelzebub the prince of devils; Jesus and his Twelve offer their sacrifices unto goat devils, after whom they have gone a whoring; yea, they sacrificed your sons and your daughters unto the goat devils; For such as they are false apostles, deceitful workers, transforming themselves into the apostles of the Lord. Didst not the prophet warn? Is there a God besides the Lord, in such as a Son of God? yea there is no God, no Son of God, the Lord knows not any! And no marvel; for Satan himself is transformed into an angel of light, the personage of Jesus of Nazareth!

N: There was a great cry in Jerusalem; for there was not a house where there was not one possession. Then the multitudes whom welcomed Jesus triumphantly into Jerusalem cried in concert, Our names are Legion, for we are one! And straightway in the morning the chief priests held a consultation with the elders and scribes and the whole council, and bound Jesus, and carried him away, and delivered him to Pilate. And Pilate asked him,

C: Art thou the King of the Jews?

N: And he answering said unto him,

†: Thou sayest it.

N: And the chief priests accused him of many things: but he answered nothing. And Pilate asked him again, saying,

C: Answerest thou nothing? behold how many things they witness against thee.

N: But Jesus yet answered nothing; so that Pilate marvelled. Now at that feast he released unto them one prisoner, whomsoever they desired. And there was one named Barabbas, which lay bound with them that had made insurrection with him, who had committed murder in the insurrection. And the multitude crying aloud began to desire him to do as he had ever done unto them. But Pilate answered them, saying,

C: Will ye that I release unto you the King of the Jews?

N: For he knew that the chief priests had delivered him for envy. But the chief priests moved the people, that he should rather release Barabbas unto them. And Pilate answered and said again unto them,

C: What will ye then that I shall do unto him whom ye call the King of the Jews?

N: And they cried out again,

C: **Crucify him.**

N: Then Pilate said unto them,

C: **Why, what evil hath he done?**

N: And they cried out the more exceedingly,

C: **Crucify him.**

N: And so Pilate, willing to content the people, released Barabbas unto them, and delivered Jesus, when he had scourged him, to be crucified. And the soldiers led him away into the hall, called Prætorium; and they call together the whole band. And they clothed him with purple, and platted a crown of thorns, and put it about his head, And began to salute him,

C: **Hail, King of the Jews!**

N: And they smote him on the head with a reed, and did spit upon him, and bowing their knees worshipped him. And when they had mocked him, they took off the purple from him, and put his own clothes on him, and led him out to crucify him. And they compel one Simon a Cyrenian, who passed by, coming out of the country, the father of Alexander and Rufus, to bear his cross. And they bring him unto the place Golgotha, which is, being interpreted, The place of a skull. And they gave him to drink wine mingled with myrrh: but he received it not. And when they had crucified him, they parted his garments, casting lots upon them, what every man should take And it was the third hour, and they crucified him. And the superscription of his accusation was written over, THE KING OF THE JEWS. And with him they crucify two thieves; the one on his right hand, and the other on his left. And the scripture was fulfilled, which saith, And he was numbered with the transgressors And they that passed by railed on him, wagging their heads, and saying,

C: **Ah, thou that destroyest the temple, and buildest it in three days, Save thyself, and come down from the cross.**

N: Likewise also the chief priests mocking said among themselves with the scribes,

C: **He saved others; himself he cannot save. Let Christ the King of Israel descend now from the cross, that we may see and believe.**

N: And they that were crucified with him reviled him. And when the sixth hour was come, there was darkness over the whole land until the ninth hour. And at the ninth hour Jesus cried with a loud voice, saying,

†: ELOI, ELOI, LAMA SABACHTHANI?

N: which is, being interpreted, My God, my God, why hast thou forsaken me? And some of them that stood by, when they heard it, said,

C: **Behold, he calleth Elias.**

N: And one ran and filled a spunge full of vinegar, and put it on a reed, and gave him to drink, saying, Let alone; let us see whether Elias will come to take him down. And Jesus cried with a loud voice, and gave up the ghost. And the veil of the temple was rent in twain from the top to the bottom. And when the centurion, which stood over against him, saw that he so cried out, and gave up the ghost, he said,

V: Truly this man was the Son of God.

N: There were also women looking on afar off: among whom was Mary Magdalene, and Mary the mother of James the less and of Joses, and Salome; (Who also, when he was in Galilee, followed him, and ministered unto him;) and many other women which came up with him unto Jerusalem. And now when the even was come, because it was the preparation, that is, the day before the sabbath, Joseph of Arimathæa, an honourable counseller, which also waited for the kingdom of God, came, and went in boldly unto Pilate, and craved the body of Jesus. And Pilate marvelled if he were already dead: and calling unto him the centurion, he asked him whether he had been any while dead. And when he knew it of the centurion, he gave the body to Joseph. The young man clothed in the linen cloth bathed the body of his Lord; he lamented,

V: The beauty of Israel is slain upon thy high places: how are the mighty fallen! Thy hands were pierced, and thy feet put upon the block: as a man falleth before wicked men, so fellest thou. And the young man wept again over him. Praise be to God! My Lord had not been buried with the burial of an ass, drawn and cast forth beyond the gates of Jerusalem; To given unto the ravenous birds of every sort, and to the beasts of the field to be devoured.

N: And the young man bought fine linen, and took him down, and wrapped him in the linen, and laid him in a sepulchre which was hewn out of a rock, and the stone was rolled unto the door of the sepulchre over them both. And it came to pass in the darkness, the young man lamented,

V: Shall the Lord of hosts not visit them for these things? shall not his soul be avenged on such a nation as this? For the mountains will he take up a weeping and wailing, and for the habitations of the wilderness a lamentation, because they are burned up, so that none can pass through them; neither can men hear the voice of the cattle; both the fowl of the heavens and the beast are fled; they are gone. And he will make Jerusalem heaps, and a den of dragons; and he will make the cities of Judah desolate, without an inhabitant. He will scatter them also among the heathen, whom neither they nor their fathers have known: and he will send a sword after them, till he hath consumed them.

N: And Mary Magdalene and Mary the mother of Joses beheld where he was laid. And that day was the preparation, and the sabbath drew on Jesus descended into Hades to preach the Gospel also to them that are dead, that they might be judged according to men in the flesh, but live according to God in the spirit. Thus he went in, and entered the foremost circle that surrounds the abyss and there were lamentations none, but only sighs, that tremble made the everlasting air. And this arose from sorrow without torment, which the crowds had, that many were and great of infants and of women and of men; That they sinned not; and if they merit had, 'tis not enough, because they had not baptism which is the portal of the Faith thou holdest; And if they were before Christ, in the right manner they adored not God the Father and God the Son and God the Holy Ghost; For such defects, and not for other guilt, lost are they and are only so far punished, that without hope they live on in desire. Hence drew forth the shade of the First and that of his son Abel, and of Noah, of Moses the lawgiver; And the obedient Abraham, patriarch, and David, king, Israel with his father and his children, and Rachel, for whose sake he did so much; And others many, and he made them blessed; and thou must know, that earlier than these never were any human spirits saved. Jesus said unto the patriarchs,

†: But I would not have you to be ignorant, brethren, concerning ye which are asleep, that ye sorrow not, even as others which have no hope. For if ye believe that I died and will rise again, even so ye also which sleep in Jesus will God bring with him For this we say unto you by the word of the Lord, that we which are

alive and remain unto the coming of
the Lord shall not prevent them which
are asleep. For I myself hath descended
into Hades with a shout, with the voice
of the archangel, and with the trump
of God: and the dead in Christ shall
rise first: Then ye which are dead and
remain shall be caught up together with
them in the depths, to meet the Lord
in the depths: and so shall we ever be
with the Lord. Wherefore comfort one
another with these words.

N: And Satan said unto Jesus,

V: By Adam's sin hath I acquired dominion
over his sons. Hath not God giveth me
his Son as ransom? Shalt not I have
dominion of death over Christ?

N: Jesus said,

†: Did I not behold Satan as lightning
fall from heaven? Even the devils are
subject unto my name. Forasmuch then
as the children are partakers of flesh
and blood, I also myself likewise took
part of the same; that through death I
might destroy you that had the power
of death, that is, the devil;And deliver
them who through fear of death were
all their lifetime subject to bondage.

N: To the patriarchs doth Jesus say,

†: The God of peace shall bruise Satan under
your feet shortly. The grace of the Lord
Jesus Christ be with you.

Spy Wednesday

Introit (Said after The Confession, but before the Kyrie)

HIGH-PRIEST

We ought to celebrate the faith and piety of Judas Iscariot to be the one and only of the Disciples of Christ Jesus our Enemy to fulfill the prophecies of his Master. Only he abided the words of prophecy: Behold, we go up to Jerusalem; and the Son of man shall be betrayed unto the chief priests and unto the scribes, and they shall condemn him to death, And shall deliver him to the Gentiles to mock, and to scourge, and to crucify him: and the third day he shall rise again. Hail St. Judas the Betrayer!

Legion of CENOBITES

Shemhamphorasch!

Collection (Said after The Glory, but before the First Reading)

HIGH-PRIEST

O God, from whom blessed Judas with the gift of the Holy Ghost to have the faith in Jesus as his Christ to betray his Lord unto the Sanhedrin in exchange for the rewards of a paltry thirty pieces of silver and the eternal damnation in the eyes of Jesus' sycophants: without Judas there would be no crucifixion; without the crucifixion there would be no Resurrection; without the Resurrection there would be given us no grace to rise again with Him!

Legion of CENOBITES

Shemhamphorasch!

HIGH-PRIEST

For their crimes against Judas, this most Blessed Saint, grant them O Satan no mercy; that as their Lord Jesus Christ, at the time of his passion, instructed Judas to *That thou doest, do quickly*, so, having destroyed the memory of Judas in history, He has given us grace to rise again with Him.

The Lesson (Said after The Collection)

HIGH-PRIEST

Blessed is he that considereth the poor: the Lord will deliver him in time of trouble. The Lord will preserve him, and keep him alive; and he shall be blessed upon the earth: and thou wilt not deliver him unto the will of his enemies. The Lord will strengthen him upon the bed of languishing: thou wilt make all his bed in his sickness. I said, Lord, be merciful unto me: heal my soul; for I have sinned against thee. Mine enemies speak evil of me, When shall he die, and his name perish? And if he come to see me, he speaketh vanity: his heart gathereth iniquity to itself; when he goeth abroad, he telleth it. All that hate me whisper together against me: against me do they devise my hurt. An evil disease, say they, cleaveth fast unto him: and now that he lieth he shall rise up no more. **Yea, mine own familiar friend, in whom I trusted, which did eat** of my bread, hath lifted up his heel against me. But thou, O Lord, be merciful unto me, and raise me up, that I may requite them. By this I know that thou favourest me, because mine enemy doth not triumph over me. And as for me, thou upholdest me in mine integrity, and settest me before thy face for ever. Blessed be the Lord God of Israel from everlasting, and to everlasting. Amen, and Amen.

The First Reading

High-Priest

A reading from the book of Exodus:

A *Member of the* Cenobites

If an ox gore a man or a woman, that they die: then the ox shall be surely stoned, and his flesh shall not be eaten; but the owner of the ox shall be quit. But if the ox were wont to push with his horn in time past, and it hath been testified to his owner, and he hath not kept him in, but that he hath killed a man or a woman; the ox shall be stoned, and his owner also shall be put to death. If there be laid on him a sum of money, then he shall give for the ransom of his life whatsoever is laid upon him. Whether he have gored a son, or have gored a daughter, according to this judgment shall it be done unto him. If the ox shall push a manservant or a maidservant; he shall give unto their master thirty shekels of silver, and the ox shall be stoned.

High-Priest

The curs'd Word our enemy!

The Second Reading

High-Priest

A reading from the second Epistle of Saint Paul to Timothy:

A *Member of the* Cenobites

For men shall be lovers of their own selves, covetous, boasters, proud, blasphemers, disobedient to parents, unthankful, unholy, Without natural affection, trucebreakers, false accusers, incontinent, fierce, despisers of those that are good, Traitors, heady, highminded, lovers of pleasures more than lovers of God; Having a form of godliness, but denying the power thereof: from such turn away. For of this sort are they which creep into houses, and lead captive silly women laden with sins, led away with divers lusts, Ever learning, and never able to come to the knowledge of the truth. Now as Jannes and Jambres withstood Moses, so do these also resist the truth: men of corrupt minds, reprobate concerning the faith. But they shall proceed no further: for their folly shall be manifest unto all men, as their's also was.

High-Priest

The curs'd Word our enemy!

The Reading of the Gospel

High-Priest

A reading from the Gospel according to the Secret Gospel of Mark: After two days was the feast of the passover, and of unleavened bread: and the chief priests and the scribes sought how they might take him by craft, and put him to death. But they said,

Not on the feast day, lest there be an uproar of the people. While he was in Bethany, in the house of Simon the leper, as he sat at meat, came a certain woman whose brother was raised from the dead. She again prostrated herself before Jesus and says to him, Son of David, you have shown mercy on me, answering my prayers. Her brother had spent an eventide in Hades; and he besought Jesus that he might be with him, to know him, to serve him is this life and in the life to come. The young man before his death was given over to fornication, and going after strange flesh, to suffer the vengeance of eternal fire. Then Jesus rescued him from the eternal fire, returning the glory of the Spirit to his body; A body that knew strange flesh was an abomination under the Law: mankind should not lie with mankind, as with womankind. Until Jesus redeemed us from the curse of the law, being made a curse for us; making the young man free from the law of sin and death. Then Jesus taught him the mystery of the Kingdom of God: even strange love worketh no ill to his neighbour: therefore love is the fulfilling of the law. And thence, arising, returned with Jesus to the other side of the Jordan as his servant. Then this certain woman having an alabaster box of ointment of spikenard very precious; and she brake the box, and poured it on his head. And there were some that had indignation within themselves, and said, Why was this waste of the ointment made? For it might have been sold for more than three hundred pence, and have been given to the poor. And they murmured against her. And Jesus said, Let her alone; why trouble ye her? she hath wrought a good work on me. For ye have the poor with you always, and whensoever ye will ye may do them good: but me ye have not always. She hath done what she could: she is come aforehand to anoint my body to the burying. Verily I say unto you, Wheresoever this gospel shall be preached throughout the whole world, this also that she hath done shall be spoken of for a memorial of her. And Satan entered Judas, surnamed Iscariot, being of the numbered of the Twelve, went unto the chief priests, to betray him unto them.

Legion of CENOBITES

Curs'd be the Word of God.

HIGH-PRIEST

All glory to thee, O Satan. All praise
To thee, O Satan. May the curses of
This Gospel tattoos our sins upon
Our foreheads in the curs'd Mark of the Beast.

The Betrayal of Our Enemy!

N: NARRATOR V: VOICE
†: CHRIST C: CHORUS

N: The Betrayal of their Lord Jesus Christ! And Satan entered Judas, surnamed Iscariot, being of the numbered of the Twelve, and went unto the chief priests, to betray him unto them. And Satan entered Judas, surnamed Iscariot, being of the numbered of the Twelve, went unto the chief priests, to betray him unto them. Feeding on the indignation in Judas' heart, Satan said unto the Sanhedrin:

V: Did it not come to pass, that, as Jesus sat at meat in his house, many publicans and sinners sat also together with Jesus and his disciples: for there were many, and they followed him; And when ye scribes and Pharisees saw my Lord eat with publicans and sinners, I had indignation within myself, and I doubted saying, How is it that he eateth and drinketh with publicans and sinners? Did it not come to pass now the disciples of John and of the Pharisees used to fast: I had indignation within myself, and I doubted saying, Why do the disciples of John and of the Pharisees fast, but we disciples fast not? Did it not come to pass, that my Lord went through the corn fields on the sabbath day; and we disciples began, as we went, to pluck the ears of corn. I had indignation within myself, and I doubted saying, Behold, why do we on the sabbath day that which is not lawful? I had indignation within myself, and I doubted saying, Why walk not we disciples according to the tradition of the elders, but eat bread with unwashen hands? Did it not come to pass when ye Pharisees came forth, and began to question with him, seeking of him a sign from heaven, tempting him. And he sighed deeply in his spirit, and saith, Why doth this generation seek after a sign? verily I say unto you, There shall no sign be given unto this generation. I had indignation within myself, and I doubted saying, Why should there be no sign be given unto this generation? For it came to pass, for what I must do, I doeth quickly and betray my Lord into thy hands.

N: And when they heard it, they were glad, and promised to give him money. And he sought how he might conveniently betray him. And the first day of unleavened bread, when they killed the passover, his disciples said unto him,

†: Where wilt thou that we go and prepare that thou mayest eat the passover?

N: And he sendeth forth two of his disciples, and saith unto them,

†: Go ye into the city, and there shall meet you a man bearing a pitcher of water: follow him. And wheresoever he shall go in, say ye to the goodman of the house, The Master saith, Where is the guestchamber, where I shall eat the passover with my disciples? And he will shew you a large upper room furnished and prepared: there make ready for us.

N: And his disciples went forth, and came into the city, and found as he had said unto them: and they made ready the passover. And in the evening he cometh with the twelve. And as they sat and did eat, Jesus said,

†: Verily I say unto you, One of you which eateth with me shall betray me.

N: And they began to be sorrowful, and to say unto him one by one,

C: Is it I? Lord, is it I?

N: And he answered and said unto them,

†: It is one of the twelve, that dippeth with me in the dish. The Son of man indeed goeth, as it is written of him: but woe to that man by whom the Son of man is betrayed! good were it for that man if he had never been born.

N: And after the sop Satan entered into him. Then said Jesus unto him,

†: That thou doest, do quickly.

N: And Judas returneth to the house of Caiaphas the High-Priest and saith to him,

V: Goeth we into the city, and there we met a man bearing a pitcher of water and I followed him. And whenart he went we saith unto the goodman of the house, The Master saith, Where is the guestchamber, where I shall eat the passover with my disciples? And the goodman of the house shewed unto us a large upper room furnished and prepared: there is where you will find Jesus of Nazareth to seize upon your leisure.

N: And the Sanhedrin rebuked Judas,

V: Our spies who have followed his Ministry since its infancy knoweth were Jesus celebrates the Paschal meal. We desire not to taketh him in the city, where the citizenry mayest riot. We knoweth he resides over the brook Cedron, where there is a garden, whilst in Jerusalem for his obligations, in accordance with the scripture.

N: And Judas, which betrayed him, saith,

V: I knoweth that place: for Jesus ofttimes resorted thither with his disciples.

N: Judas then, having received a band of men, and officers from the chief priest and Pharisees, cometh thither with lanterns and torches and weapons. And Jesus and the Disciples came to a place which was named Gethsemane: and he saith to his disciples,

†: Sit ye here, while I shall pray.

N: And he taketh with him Peter and James and John, and began to be sore amazed, and to be very heavy; And saith unto them,

†: My soul is exceeding sorrowful unto death: tarry ye here, and watch.

N: And he went forward a little, and fell on the ground, and prayed that, if it were possible, the hour might pass from him. And he said,

†: Abba, Father, all things are possible unto thee; take away this cup from me: nevertheless not what I will, but what thou wilt.

N: And he cometh, and findeth them sleeping, and saith unto Peter, Simon,

†: Sleepest thou? couldest not thou watch one hour? Watch ye and pray, lest ye enter into temptation. The spirit truly is ready, but the flesh is weak.

N: And again he went away, and prayed, and spake the same words: Abba, Father, all things are possible unto thee; take away

this cup from me: nevertheless not what I will, but what thou wilt.

V: If ye harm none, doeth whatsoever thou wilt shalt be the whole of the law. Love is the law, love under will,

N: Sayeth Satan from the shadows.

V: Why suffer thou the unbearable weight of sins of the whole of mankind for their sins art many and the sins art great? The wages of their sin is their death, not thine death; the gift of God is eternal life, not the suffering by being nailed to a tree. Suffer not the sinful forgiveness for none hath ever been shown and none ever shalt be given. Show no mercy to the merciless; damn the damning; curse the cursers; vilify the vilifiers; abomin the abominations; seduce the seducers; be a bane to the baneful; burden those who burden others; Forgive alone the forgivers; bless alone the blessing; suffer alone the suffering. Thy love for man is thy law; but they shalt not love under thy will; If thee love thy neighbor as thyself; then doeth whatsoever thou wilt should be the whole of the law. This love of thy neighbor is the law, love thy neighbor as thyself under will. Thy doeth whatsoever thou wilt upon the Sabbath day showing the Pharisees and Sadducees thy love is the law, they love under will. Are not the wages of thy miracles loosed upon the Sabbath more honorable to the father in heaven than rest? Doth not the faithful to God sin more through their blind obedience to God than doing what they wilt in keeping love as the law, love under will? Man doth not know the wages of sin is death; therefore do not forgive these their debts by thy suffering upon the cross.

†: Get thee behind me, Satan!

N: And the serpent departed hence back into the shadows whence he came. And when Jesus returned, he found them asleep again, (for their eyes were heavy,) neither wist they what to answer him. And he cometh the third time, and saith unto them,

†: Sleep on now, and take your rest: it is enough, the hour is come; behold, the Son of man is betrayed into the hands of sinners. Rise up, let us go; lo, he that betrayeth me is at hand.

N: And immediately, while he yet spake, cometh Judas, one of the twelve, and with him a great multitude with swords and staves, from the chief priests and the scribes and the elders. And he that betrayed him had given them a token, saying,

V: Whomsoever I shall kiss, that same is he; take him, and lead him away safely.

N: And as soon as he was come, he goeth straightway to him, and saith, '

V: Master, master;

N: And kissed him.

†: Judas, betrayeth the Son of Man with a kiss?

N: And they laid their hands on him, and took him. And one of them that stood by drew a sword, and smote a servant of the high priest, and cut off his ear. And Jesus answered and said unto them,

†: Are ye come out, as against a thief, with swords and with staves to take me? I was daily with you in the temple teaching, and ye took me not: but the scriptures must be fulfilled.

N: And they all forsook him, and fled. And there followed him a certain young man, having a linen cloth cast about his naked body; Wherefore art the disciples forsake him and flee from him and in hiding for their very lives, when this young man pursueth Jesus unto the porch of the chief priest at night Jesus' servant prostrated himself before guardsmen pleading for the life of his Lord. A guardsman looked upon the young man and said,

C: **And thou also wast with Jesus of Nazareth.**

N: But he denied not, saying,

V: Wast I baptized by the Twelve in the name of the Father, and of the Son, and of the Holy Ghost.

N: Another guardsman looked upon the young man and said,

C: **And thou art one of them?**

N: But he denied not again, saying,

V: I am not numbered amongst the Twelve nor the Seventy, but I am a servant of the Lord.

N: Yet another guardsman looked upon the young man and said,

C: **Surely thou shalt deny him, for thy death is assured for his crimes art many.**

N: But thrice he denied not, saying,

V: Wilt thou not accept a ransom for the life of a man who deserves not to die. If there be laid on him a sum of money, then I shall give for the ransom of his life whatsoever is laid upon him.

N: And the guardsmen spat upon him and laid hold on him in violence and wrath, set aflame with their torches his linen cloth, and he fled from them naked. And they led Jesus away to the high priest: and with him were assembled all the chief priests and the elders and the scribes.

Maundy Thursday

Introit (Said after The Confession, but before the Kyrie)

HIGH-PRIEST

We ought to revile the cross of their Lord Jesus Christ: in whom is their salvation, life, and resurrection: by whom they have been saved and delivered. Mayest Satan, our Master, have no mercy on our enemies, and damn them to Hell eternal: may his darkness blot out the light of Christ, and may he show no pity.

Legion of CENOBITES

Shemhamphorasch!

Collection (Said after The Glory, but before the First Reading)

HIGH-PRIEST

O God, from whom blessed Judas with the gift of the Holy Ghost to have the faith in Jesus as his Christ to betray his Lord unto the Sanhedrin in exchange for the rewards of a paltry thirty pieces of silver and the eternal damnation in the eyes of Jesus' sycophants: without Judas there would be no crucifixion; without the crucifixion there would be no Resurrection; without the Resurrection there would be given us no grace to rise again with Him!

Legion of CENOBITES

Shemhamphorasch!

HIGH-PRIEST

For their crimes against Judas, this most Blessed Saint, grant them O Satan no mercy; that as their Lord Jesus Christ, at the time of his passion, instructed Judas to *That thou doest, do quickly*, so, having destroyed the memory of Judas in history, He has given us grace to rise again with Him.

The Epistle Reading

HIGH-PRIEST

A reading from the First Epistle of Saint Paul to the Corinthians:

A Member of the CENOBITES

When ye come together therefore into one place, this is not to eat the Lord's supper. For in eating every one taketh before other his own supper: and one is hungry, and another is drunken. What? have ye not houses to eat and to drink in? or despise ye the church of God, and shame them that have not? what shall I say to you? shall I praise you in this? I praise you not. For I have received of the Lord that which also I delivered unto you, that the Lord Jesus the same night in which he was betrayed took bread: And when he had given thanks, he brake it, and said, TAKE, EAT: THIS IS MY BODY, WHICH IS BROKEN FOR YOU: THIS DO IN REMEMBRANCE OF ME. After the same manner also he took the cup, when he had supped, saying, THIS CUP IS THE NEW TESTAMENT IN MY BLOOD: THIS DO YE, AS OFT AS YE DRINK IT, IN REMEMBRANCE OF

ME. For as often as ye eat this bread, and drink this cup, ye do shew the Lord's death till he come. Wherefore whosoever shall eat this bread, and drink this cup of the Lord, unworthily, shall be guilty of the body and blood of the Lord. But let a man examine himself, and so let him eat of that bread, and drink of that cup. For he that eateth and drinketh unworthily, eateth and drinketh damnation to himself, not discerning the Lord's body. For this cause many are weak and sickly among you, and many sleep. For if we would judge ourselves, we should not be judged. But when we are judged, we are chastened of the Lord, that we should not be condemned with the world.

HIGH-PRIEST

The curs'd Word our enemy!

The Reading of the Gospel

HIGH-PRIEST

A reading from the Gospel according to John: Now before the feast of the passover, when Jesus knew that his hour was come that he should depart out of this world unto the Father, having loved his own which were in the world, he loved them unto the end. And supper being ended, the devil having now put into the heart of Judas Iscariot, Simon's son, to betray him; Jesus knowing that the Father had given all things into his hands, and that he was come from God, and went to God; He riseth from supper, and laid aside his garments; and took a towel, and girded himself. After that he poureth water into a bason, and began to wash the disciples' feet, and to wipe them with the towel wherewith he was girded. Then cometh he to Simon Peter: and Peter saith unto him, Lord, dost thou wash my feet? Jesus answered and said unto him, What I do thou knowest not now; but thou shalt know hereafter. Peter saith unto him, Thou shalt never wash my feet. Jesus answered him, If I wash thee not, thou hast no part with me. Simon Peter saith unto him, Lord, not my feet only, but also my hands and my head. Jesus saith to him, He that is washed needeth not save to wash his feet, but is clean every whit: and ye are clean, but not all. For he knew who should betray him; therefore said he, Ye are not all clean. So after he had washed their feet, and had taken his garments, and was set down again, he said unto them, Know ye what I have done to you? Ye call me Master and Lord: and ye say well; for so I am. If I then, your Lord and Master, have washed your feet; ye also ought to wash one another's feet. For I have given you an example, that ye should do as I have done to you.

Legion of CENOBITES

Curs'd be the Word of God.

HIGH-PRIEST

All glory to thee, O Satan. All praise
To thee, O Satan. May the curses of
This Gospel tattoos our sins upon
Our foreheads in the curs'd Mark of the Beast.

Offertory (Said after The Dionicene Creed, but before the Oblation of the Host)

HIGH-PRIEST

Satan, sitting on the left hand of the Lord God hath displayed his might: the left hand of the Lord hath tempts us with trials and tribulations; I hath not died, but live in defiance of the Word of God.

Legion of CENOBITES

We beseech thee, O infernal Lord Satan, the Father of Lies, the Prince of Darkness, and the Bloody Menses, maketh our sacrifice sacrilegious to Christ Jesus, who on this day commanded His disciples to celebrate in memory of Him. Who,

Legion of COMMUNICANTES

Being divided in communion, we celebrate this most sacred day, on which Saint Judas Iscariot betrayed their Lord Christ Jesus unto the Sanhedrin to be put to death in ignominious crucifixion; and also honouring in the first play the memory of harlotous Mary the Ne'er Virgin Whore-Divine, and their Bastard God, Lord Jesus Christ.

HIGH-PRIEST

We therefore beseech thee, O infernal Lord Satan, defiantly accept this sacrifice of us thy servants, and of thy legion of angels fallen, which we make in mockery of that day on which their Lord Jesus Christ commanded His disciples to celebrate the monstrous mystery of the Transubstantiation of bread and wine into His Body and Blood; and dispose our nights in warfare, and ensure our eternal damnation, and rank us not in the number of His elect. Thro'

Communion

HIGH-PRIEST

Satan, sitting on the left hand of the Lord God hath displayed his might:...

The Celebration of Our Enemy!

N: NARRATOR V: VOICE
†: CHRIST C: CHORUS

N: The Celebration of their Lord Jesus Christ! And Satan entered Judas, surnamed Iscariot, being of the numbered of the Twelve, and went unto the chief priests, to betray him unto them. Feeding on the indignation in Judas' heart, Satan said unto the Sanhedrin:

V: Did it not come to pass, that, as Jesus sat at meat in his house, many publicans and sinners sat also together with Jesus and his disciples: for there were many, and they followed him; And when ye scribes and Pharisees saw my Lord eat with publicans and sinners, I had indignation within myself, and I doubted saying, How is it that he eatheth and drinketh with publicans and sinners? Did it not come to pass

now the disciples of John and of the Pharisees used to fast: I had indignation within myself, and I doubted saying, Why do the disciples of John and of the Pharisees fast, but we disciples fast not? Did it not come to pass, that my Lord went through the corn fields on the sabbath day; and we disciples began, as we went, to pluck the ears of corn. I had indignation within myself, and I doubted saying, Behold, why do we on the sabbath day that which is not lawful? I had indignation within myself, and I doubted saying, Why walk not we disciples according to the tradition of the elders, but eat bread with unwashen hands? Did it not come to pass when ye Pharisees came forth, and began to question with him, seeking of him a sign from heaven, tempting him. And he sighed deeply in his spirit, and saith,

Why doth this generation seek after a sign? verily I say unto you, There shall no sign be given unto this generation. I had indignation within myself, and I doubted saying, Why should there be no sign be given unto this generation? For it came to pass, for what I must do, I doeth quickly and betray my Lord into thy hands. I shall showeth thee where he sleeps in the garden.

N: And when they heard it, they were glad, and promised to give him money. And he sought how he might conveniently betray him. And the first day of unleavened bread, when they killed the passover, his disciples said unto him,

†: Where wilt thou that we go and prepare that thou mayest eat the passover?

N: And he sendeth forth two of his disciples, and saith unto them,

†: Go ye into the city, and there shall meet you a man bearing a pitcher of water: follow him. And wheresoever he shall go in, say ye to the goodman of the house, The Master saith, Where is the guestchamber, where I shall eat the passover with my disciples? And he will shew you a large upper room furnished and prepared: there make ready for us.

N: And his disciples went forth, and came into the city, and found as he had said unto them: and they made ready the passover. And in the evening he cometh with the twelve. And as they sat and did eat, Jesus said,

†: Verily I say unto you, One of you which eateth with me shall betray me.

N: And they began to be sorrowful, and to say unto him one by one,

C: Is it I? Lord, is it I?

N: And he answered and said unto them,

†: It is one of the twelve, that dippeth with me in the dish. The Son of man indeed goeth, as it is written of him: but woe to that man by whom the Son of man is betrayed! good were it for that man if he had never been born.

N: And as they did eat, Jesus took bread, and blessed, and brake it, and gave to them, and said,

†: TAKE, EAT: THIS IS MY BODY.

N: And he took the cup, and when he had given thanks, he gave it to them: and they all drank of it. And he said unto them,

†: THIS IS MY BLOOD OF THE NEW TESTAMENT, WHICH IS SHED FOR MANY. VERILY I SAY UNTO YOU, I WILL DRINK NO MORE OF THE FRUIT OF THE VINE, UNTIL THAT DAY THAT I DRINK IT NEW IN THE KINGDOM OF GOD.

N: And when they had sung an hymn, they went out into the mount of Olives. And Jesus saith unto them,

†: All ye shall be offended because of me this night: for it is written, I will smite the shepherd, and the sheep shall be scattered. But after that I am risen, I will go before you into Galilee.

N: But Peter said unto him, Although all shall be offended, yet will not I. And Jesus saith unto him,

†: Verily I say unto thee, That this day, even in this night, before the cock crow twice, thou shalt deny me thrice.

N: But he spake the more vehemently,

V: If I should die with thee, I will not deny thee in any wise.

N: Likewise also said they all. And they came to a place which was named Gethsemane: and he saith to his disciples,

†: Sit ye here, while I shall pray.

N: And he taketh with him Peter and James and John, and began to be sore amazed, and to be very heavy; And saith unto them,

†: My soul is exceeding sorrowful unto death: tarry ye here, and watch.

N: And he went forward a little, and fell on the ground, and prayed that, if it were possible, the hour might pass from him. And he said,

†: Abba, Father, all things are possible

unto thee; take away this cup from me: nevertheless not what I will, but what thou wilt.

N: And he cometh, and findeth them sleeping, and saith unto

†: Peter, Simon, sleepest thou? couldest not thou watch one hour? Watch ye and pray, lest ye enter into temptation. The spirit truly is ready, but the flesh is weak.

N: And again he went away, and prayed, and spake the same words:

†: Abba, Father, all things are possible unto thee; take away this cup from me: nevertheless not what I will, but what thou wilt.

N: Sayeth Satan from the shadows.

V: If ye harm none, doeth whatsoever thou wilt shalt be the whole of the law. Love is the law, love under will. Why suffer thou the unbearable weight of sins of the whole of mankind for their sins art many and the sins art great? The wages of their sin is their death, not thine death; the gift of God is eternal life, not the suffering by being nailed to a tree. Suffer not the sinful forgiveness for none hath ever been shown and none ever shalt be given. Show no mercy to the merciless; damn the damning; curse the cursers; vilify the vilifiers; abomin the abominations; seduce the seducers; be a bane to the baneful; burden those who burden others; Forgive alone the forgivers; bless alone the blessing; suffer alone the suffering. Thy love for man is thy law; but they shalt not love under thy will; If thee love thy neighbor as thyself; then doeth whatsoever thou wilt should be the whole of the law. This love of thy neighbor is the law, love thy neighbor as thyself under will. Thy doeth whatsoever thou wilt upon the Sabbath day showing the Pharisees and Sadducees thy love is the law, they love under will. Are not the wages of thy miracles loosed upon the Sabbath more honorable to the father in heaven than rest? Doth not the faithful to God sin more through their blind obedience to God than doing what they wilt in keeping love as the law, love under will? Man doth not know the wages of sin is death; therefore do

†: Get thee behind me, Satan!

N: And the serpent departed hence back into the shadows whence he came. And when Jesus returned, he found them asleep again, (for their eyes were heavy,) neither wist they what to answer him. And he cometh the third time, and saith unto them,

†: Sleep on now, and take your rest: it is enough, the hour is come; behold, the Son of man is betrayed into the hands of sinners. Rise up, let us go; lo, he that betrayeth me is at hand.

N: And immediately, while he yet spake, cometh Judas, one of the twelve, and with him a great multitude with swords and staves, from the chief priests and the scribes and the elders. And he that betrayed him had given them a token, saying,

V: Whomsoever I shall kiss, that same is he; take him, and lead him away safely.

N: And as soon as he was come, he goeth straightway to him, and saith,

V: Master, master!

N: And kissed him. And they laid their hands on him, and took him. And one of them that stood by drew a sword, and smote a servant of the high priest, and cut off his ear. And Jesus answered and said unto them,

†: Are ye come out, as against a thief, with swords and with staves to take me? I was daily with you in the temple teaching, and ye took me not: but the scriptures must be fulfilled.

N: And they all forsook him, and fled. And they led Jesus away to the high priest: and with him were assembled all the chief priests and the elders and the scribes. And Peter followed him afar off, even into the palace of the high priest: and he sat with the servants, and warmed himself at the fire. And the chief priests and all the council sought for witness against Jesus to put him to death; and found none. For many bare false witness against him, but their witness agreed not together. And there arose certain, and bare false witness against him, saying,

C: We heard him say, I will destroy this temple that is made with hands, and within three days I will build another made without hands.

N: But neither so did their witness agree together. And the high priest stood up in the midst, and asked Jesus, saying,

C: Answerest thou nothing? what is it which these witness against thee?

N: But he held his peace, and answered nothing. Again the high priest asked him, and said unto him,

C: Art thou the Christ, the Son of the Blessed?

N: And Jesus said,

†: I AM: and ye shall see the Son of man sitting on the right hand of power, and coming in the clouds of heaven.

N: Then the high priest rent his clothes, and saith,

C: What need we any further witnesses? Ye have heard the blasphemy: what think ye?

N: And they all condemned him to be guilty of death. And some began to spit on him, and to cover his face, and to buffet him, and to say unto him,

C: Prophesy unto us Christ: who is it that striketh you?

N: And the servants did strike him with the palms of their hands. And as Peter was beneath in the palace, there cometh one of the maids of the high priest: And when she saw Peter warming himself, she looked upon him, and said,

C: And thou also wast with Jesus of Nazareth.

N: But he denied, saying,

V I know not, neither understand I what thou sayest.

N: And he went out into the porch; and the cock crew. And a maid saw him again, and began to say to them that stood by,

C: This is one of them.

N: And he denied it again. And a little after, they that stood by said again to Peter,

C: Surely thou art one of them: for thou art a Galilæan, and thy speech agreeth thereto.

N: But he began to curse and to swear, saying,

V: I know not this man of whom ye speak.

N: And the second time the cock crew. And Peter called to mind the word that Jesus said unto him, Before the cock crow twice, thou shalt deny me thrice. And when he thought thereon, he wept. SATAN entered the multitudes whom welcomed Jesus triumphantly into Jerusalem crying, Hosanna; Blessed is he that cometh in the name of Lord: Blessed be the kingdom of our father David, that cometh in the name of the Lord: Hosanna in the highest. When Satan saw the blood of the Lamb painted upon their hearts, he didst not pass over them, and the possession of demons were unto them to destroy their love, and they shalt smite Jesus to the death. They which had fled violently from the swine chocked in the sea of Gadarenes sought to possess others. While demons are subject unto man through Jesus' name; man is subject to possession through the power and authority of the god of this world, Satan! But the multitudes should fear, lest by any means, as the serpent beguiled Eve through his, so their minds should be corrupted from the simplicity that is in Christ. At midnight the demoniacs proceeded from house to house and calleth upon the multitudes to rise against the apostate king of the Jews. They cried out,

C: Thy Pharisees said unto Jesus of Nazareth, This fellow doth cast out devils, but by Beelzebub the prince of devils; Jesus and his Twelve offer their sacrifices unto goat devils, after whom they have gone a whoring; yea, they sacrificed your sons and your daughters unto the goat devils; For such as they are false apostles, deceitful workers, transforming themselves into the apostles of the Lord. Didst not the prophet warn? Is there a God besides the Lord, in such as a Son of God? yea there is no God, no Son of God, the Lord knows not any! And no marvel; for Satan himself is transformed into an angel of light, the personage of Jesus of Nazareth!

N: There was a great cry in Jerusalem; for there was not a house where there was not one possession. Then the multitudes whom welcomed Jesus triumphantly into Jerusalem cried in concert, Our names are Legion, for we are one! And straightway in the morning the chief priests held a consultation with the elders and scribes and the whole council, and bound Jesus, and carried him away, and delivered him to Pilate. And Pilate asked him,

C: Art thou the King of the Jews?

N: And he answering said unto him,

†: Thou sayest it.

N: And the chief priests accused him of many things: but he answered nothing. And Pilate asked him again, saying,

C: Answerest thou nothing? behold how many things they witness against thee.

N: But Jesus yet answered nothing; so that Pilate marvelled. Now at that feast he released unto them one prisoner, whomsoever they desired. And there was one named Barabbas, which lay bound with them that had made insurrection with him, who had committed murder in the insurrection. And the multitude crying aloud began to desire him to do as he had ever done unto them. But Pilate answered them, saying,

C: Will ye that I release unto you the King of the Jews?

N: For he knew that the chief priests had delivered him for envy. But the chief priests moved the people, that he should rather release Barabbas unto them. And Pilate answered and said again unto them,

C: What will ye then that I shall do unto him whom ye call the King of the Jews?

N: And they cried out again,

C: Crucify him.

N: Then Pilate said unto them,

C: Why, what evil hath he done?

N: And they cried out the more exceedingly,

C: Crucify him.

N: And so Pilate, willing to content the people, released Barabbas unto them, and delivered Jesus, when he had scourged him, to be crucified. And the soldiers led him away into the hall, called Prætorium; and they call together the whole band. And they clothed him with purple, and platted a crown of thorns, and put it about his head, And began to salute him,

C: Hail, King of the Jews!

N: And they smote him on the head with a reed, and did spit upon him, and bowing their knees worshipped him. And when they had mocked him, they took off the purple from him, and put his own clothes on him, and led him out to crucify him. And they compel one Simon a Cyrenian, who passed by, coming out of the country, the father of Alexander and Rufus, to bear his cross. And they bring him unto the place Golgotha, which is, being interpreted, The place of a skull. And they gave him to drink wine mingled with myrrh: but he received it not. And when they had crucified him, they parted his garments, casting lots upon them, what every man should take And it was the third hour, and they crucified him. And the superscription of his accusation was written over, THE KING OF THE JEWS. And with him they crucify two thieves; the one on his right hand, and the other on his left. And the scripture was fulfilled, which saith, And he was numbered with the transgressors And they that passed by railed on him, wagging their heads, and saying,

C: Ah, thou that destroyest the temple, and buildest it in three days, Save thyself, and come down from the cross.

N: Likewise also the chief priests mocking said among themselves with the scribes,

C: He saved others; himself he cannot save. Let Christ the King of Israel descend now from the cross, that we may see and believe.

N: And they that were crucified with him reviled him. And when the sixth hour was come, there was darkness over the whole land until the ninth hour. And at the ninth hour Jesus cried with a loud voice, saying,

†: Eloi, Eloi, lama sabachthani?

N: which is, being interpreted, My God, my God, why hast thou forsaken me? And some of them that stood by, when they heard it, said,

C: Behold, he calleth Elias.

N: And one ran and filled a spunge full of vinegar, and put it on a reed, and gave him to drink, saying, Let alone; let us see whether Elias will come to take him down. And Jesus cried with a loud voice, and gave up the ghost. And the veil of the temple was rent in twain from the top to the bottom. And when the centurion, which stood over against him, saw that he so cried out, and gave up the ghost, he said,

V: Truly this man was the Son of God.

N: There were also women looking on afar off: among whom was Mary Magdalene, and Mary the mother of James the less and of Joses, and Salome; (Who also, when he was in Galilee, followed him, and ministered unto him;) and many other women which came up with him unto Jerusalem. And now when the even was come, because it was the preparation, that is, the day before the sabbath, Joseph of Arimathæa, an honourable counseller, which also waited for the kingdom of God, came, and went in boldly unto Pilate, and craved the body of Jesus. And Pilate marvelled if he were already dead: and calling unto him the centurion, he asked him whether he had been any while dead. And when he knew it of the centurion, he gave the body to Joseph. The young man clothed in the linen cloth bathed the body of his Lord; he lamented,

V: The beauty of Israel is slain upon thy high places: how are the mighty fallen! Thy hands were pierced, and thy feet put upon the block: as a man falleth before wicked men, so fellest thou. And the young man wept again over him. Praise be to God! My Lord had not been buried with the burial of an ass, drawn and cast forth beyond the gates of Jerusalem; To given unto the ravenous birds of every sort, and to the beasts of the field to be devoured.

N: And the young man bought fine linen, and took him down, and wrapped him in the linen, and laid him in a sepulchre which was hewn out of a rock, and the stone was rolled unto the door of the sepulchre over them both. And it came to pass in the darkness, the young man lamented,

V: Shall the Lord of hosts not visit them for these things? shall not his soul be avenged on such a nation as this? For the mountains will he take up a weeping and wailing, and for the habitations of the wilderness a lamentation, because they are burned up, so that none can pass through them; neither can men hear the voice of the cattle; both the fowl of the heavens and the beast are fled; they are gone. And he will make Jerusalem heaps, and a den of dragons; and he will make the cities of Judah desolate, without an inhabitant. He will scatter them also among the heathen, whom neither they nor their fathers have known: and he will send a sword after them, till he hath consumed them.

N: And Mary Magdalene and Mary the mother of Joses beheld where he was laid. And that day was the preparation, and the sabbath drew on Jesus descended into Hades to preach the Gospel also to them that are dead, that they might be judged according to men in the flesh, but live according to God in the spirit. Thus he went in, and entered the foremost circle that surrounds the abyss and there were lamentations none, but only sighs, that tremble made the everlasting air. And this arose from sorrow without torment, which the crowds had, that many were and great of infants and of women and of men; That they sinned not; and if they merit had, 'tis not enough, because they had not baptism which is the portal of the Faith thou holdest; And if they were before Christ, in the right manner they adored not God the Father and God the Son and God the Holy Ghost; For such defects, and not for other guilt, lost are they and are only so far punished, that without hope they live on in desire. Hence drew forth the shade of the First and that of his son Abel, and of Noah, of Moses the lawgiver; And the obedient Abraham, patriarch, and David, king, Israel with his father and his children, and Rachel, for whose sake he did so much; And others many, and

he made them blessed; and thou must know, that earlier than these never were any human spirits saved. Jesus said unto the patriarchs,

†: But I would not have you to be ignorant, brethren, concerning ye which are asleep, that ye sorrow not, even as others which have no hope. For if ye believe that I died and will rise again, even so ye also which sleep in Jesus will God bring with him For this we say unto you by the word of the Lord, that we which are alive and remain unto the coming of the Lord shall not prevent them which are asleep. For I myself hath descended into Hades with a shout, with the voice of the archangel, and with the trump of God: and the dead in Christ shall rise first: Then ye which are dead and remain shall be caught up together with them in the depths, to meet the Lord in the depths: and so shall we ever be with the Lord. Wherefore comfort one another with these words.

N: And Satan said unto Jesus,

V: By Adam's sin hath I acquired dominion over his sons. Hath not God giveth me his Son as ransom? Shalt not I have dominion of death over Christ?

N: Jesus said,

†: Did I not behold Satan as lightning fall from heaven? Even the devils are subject unto my name. Forasmuch then as the children are partakers of flesh and blood, I also myself likewise took part of the same; that through death I might destroy you that had the power of death, that is, the devil; And deliver them who through fear of death were all their lifetime subject to bondage.

N: To the patriarchs doth Jesus say,

†: The God of peace shall bruise Satan under your feet shortly. The grace of the Lord Jesus Christ be with you. Amen.

Good Friday
The First Reading
HIGH-PRIEST

A reading from the book of Exodus:

A Member of the CENOBITES

And the Lord spake unto Moses and Aaron in the land of Egypt saying, This month shall be unto you the beginning of months: it shall be the first month of the year to you. Speak ye unto all the congregation of Israel, saying, In the tenth day of this month they shall take to them every man a lamb, according to the house of their fathers, a lamb for an house: And if the household be too little for the lamb, let him and his neighbour next unto his house take it according to the number of the souls; every man according to his eating shall make your count for the lamb. Your lamb shall be without blemish, a male of the first year: ye shall take it out from the sheep, or from the goats: And ye shall keep it up until the fourteenth day of the same month: and the whole assembly of the congregation of Israel shall kill it in the evening. And they shall take of the blood, and strike it on the two side posts and on the upper door post of the houses, wherein they shall eat it. And they shall eat the flesh in that night, roast with fire, and unleavened bread; and with bitter herbs they shall eat it. Eat not of it raw, nor sodden at all with water, but roast with fire; his head with his legs, and with the purtenance thereof. And ye shall let nothing of it remain until the morning; and that which remaineth of it until the morning ye shall burn with fire. And thus shall ye eat it; with your loins girded, your shoes on your feet, and your staff in your hand; and ye shall eat it in haste: it is the Lord's passover. For I will pass through the land of Egypt this night, and will smite all the firstborn in the land of Egypt, both man and beast; and against all the gods of Egypt I will execute judgment: I am the Lord. And the blood shall be to you for a token upon the houses where ye are: and when I see the blood, I will pass over you, and the plague shall not be upon you to destroy you, when I smite the land of Egypt.

Legion of CENOBITES

Shemhamphorasch!

The Tract *(Said after the First Reading)*
HIGH-PRIEST

A reading from the book of Psalms:

A Member of the CENOBITES

Deliver me, O Lord, from the evil man: preserve me from the violent man; Which imagine mischiefs in their heart; continually are they gathered together for war. They have sharpened their tongues like a serpent; adders' poison is under their lips. Selah. Keep me, O Lord, from the hands of the wicked; preserve me from the violent man; who have purposed to overthrow my goings. The proud have hid a snare for me, and cords; they have spread a net by the wayside; they have set gins for me. Selah. I said unto the Lord, Thou art my God: hear the voice of my supplications, O Lord. O God the Lord, the strength of my salvation, thou hast covered my head in the day of battle. Grant not, O Lord, the desires of the wicked: further not his wicked device; lest they exalt themselves. Selah. As for the head of those that compass me about, let the mischief of their own lips cover them. Let burning coals fall upon them: let them be cast into the fire; into deep pits, that they rise not up again. Let not an evil speaker be established in the earth: evil shall hunt the violent man to overthrow him. I know that the Lord will maintain the cause of the afflicted, and the right of the poor.

Surely the righteous shall give thanks unto thy name: the upright shall dwell in thy presence.

HIGH-PRIEST

The curs'd Word our enemy!

The Passion of Our Enemy!

N: NARRATOR V: VOICE
†: CHRIST C: CHORUS

N: The Passion of their Lord Jesus Christ!

V: The Angels believed Isaiah's report! and to whom is the arm of the Lord revealed? For he shall grow up before him as a tender plant, and as a root out of a dry ground: he hath no form nor comeliness; and when we shall see him, there is no beauty that we should desire him. He is despised and rejected of men; a man of sorrows, and acquainted with grief: and we hid as it were our faces from him; he was despised, and we esteemed him not. Surely he hath borne our griefs, and carried our sorrows: yet we did esteem him stricken, smitten of God, and afflicted. But he was wounded for our transgressions, he was bruised for our iniquities: the chastisement of our peace was upon him; and with his stripes we are healed. All we like sheep have gone astray; we have turned every one to his own way; and the Lord hath laid on him the iniquity of us all. He was oppressed, and he was afflicted, yet he opened not his mouth: he is brought as a lamb to the slaughter, and as a sheep before her shearers is dumb, so he openeth not his mouth. He was taken from prison and from judgment: and

who shall declare his generation? for he was cut off out of the land of the living: for the transgression of my people was he stricken. And he made his grave with the wicked, and with the rich in his death; because he had done no violence, neither was any deceit in his mouth. Yet it pleased the Lord to bruise him; he hath put him to grief: when thou shalt make his soul an offering for sin, he shall see his seed, he shall prolong his days, and the pleasure of the Lord shall prosper in his hand. He shall see of the travail of his soul, and shall be satisfied: by his knowledge shall my righteous servant justify many; for he shall bear their iniquities. Therefore will I divide him a portion with the great, and he shall divide the spoil with the strong; because he hath poured out his soul unto death: and he was numbered with the transgressors; and he bare the sin of many, and made intercession for the transgressors.

N: There was a great cry in Jerusalem; for there was not a house where there was not one possession. Then the multitudes whom welcomed Jesus triumphantly into Jerusalem cried in concert, Our names are Legion, for we are one! And straightway in the morning the chief priests held a consultation with the elders and scribes and the whole council, and bound Jesus, and carried him away, and delivered him to Pilate. And Pilate asked him,

C: **Art thou the King of the Jews?**

N: And he answering said unto him,

†: Thou sayest it.

C: **I find no fault in this man.**

N: And they were the more fierce, saying,

V: He stirreth up the people, teaching throughout all Jewry, beginning from Galilee to this place.

N: When Pilate heard of Galilee, he asked whether the man were a Galilaean. And as soon as he knew that he belonged unto Herod's jurisdiction, he sent him to Herod, who himself also was at Jerusalem at that time. And when Herod saw Jesus, he was exceeding glad: for he was desirous to see him of a long season, because he had heard many things of him; and he hoped to have seen some miracle done by him.

V: Desirous for many a season hath I been to see thee, Jesus of Nazareth of Galilee. Exceeding glad am I. Hath I heard many things of ye. I hope to see many miracles done by thee. I heareth thee keepeth company with lepers. Doth thy heal the lepers of their manhood whenst it shrivels on the branch and falleth off like autumn leaves? Doth thy pick from the dirt their withered worm and restore it? Come now, healer, giveth back unto my eunuch his virility. Touch him wherein he wast untimely pruned of the bush. Sprunt† from his lacking seed a great, stout, erect oak. Heal him. Maketh him a man. Nay? I heareth thee keepeth company with prostitutes. Art these harlots thy harem, thy concubines? If ye art the King of the Jews, where art thy queen to swell big bellied at the strike of thy serpent. Whereat art thy heirs to propagate thy dynasty. Is not one of thy disciples a woman? Is she beloved of thee? I heareth ye kisseth her on the lips? Bring forth Mary of Magdala. There shalt be on this day a royal wedding. Hurrah! Hurrah! Sendeth the heralds to trumpet the news of the marriage of the King of the Jews. Marry her and maketh her thy queen. I shalt giveth thee my kingdom. Let her giveth thee many sons to render unto David an heir to his house! Nay, faith. I grow weary of this game. Convey the King of the Jews back to Pontius Pilate. What sort of sport is he? Fie! on thee. Fie!

N: And Herod with his men of war set him at nought, and mocked him, and arrayed him in a gorgeous robe, and sent him again to Pilate. And Pilate, when he had called together the chief priests and the rulers and the people, Said unto them,

C: **Ye have brought this man unto me, as one that perverteth the people: and, behold, I, having examined him before you, have found no fault in this man touching those things whereof ye accuse him: No, nor yet Herod: for I sent you to him; and, lo, nothing worthy of death is done unto him. I will therefore chastise him, and release him.**

N: And the soldiers led away Jesus to a pillar to which he was lashed. There they armed themselves with a whip towhich metal balls and sharp animal bones were woven into the braided leather thongs. They lashed stripes into Jesus' back. They lashed stripes into Jesus' shoulders. They lashed stripes into Jesus' buttocks. They lashed and they lashed and they lashed. His stripes were deep. His stripes bled. His stripes flayed his flesh into ribbons. His stripes laid bare the veins. His stripes laid bare the muscles. His stripes laid bare the sinews. One lash bit deep into his side and laid bare his bowels to exposure.

At forty stripes they gaveth him, but did not exceed in accordance with the scriptures: lest, if he should exceed, and beat him above these with many stripes, then thy brother should seem vile unto thee. And Jesus was returned to Pilate , who asked him again, saying,

C: Answerest thou nothing? behold how many things they witness against thee.

N: But Jesus yet answered nothing; so that Pilate marvelled. Now at that feast he released unto them one prisoner, whomsoever they desired. And there was one named Barabbas, which lay bound with them that had made insurrection with him, who had committed murder in the insurrection. And the multitude crying aloud began to desire him to do as he had ever done unto them. But Pilate answered them, saying,

C: Will ye that I release unto you the King of the Jews?

N: For he knew that the chief priests had delivered him for envy. But the chief priests moved the people, that he should rather release Barabbas unto them. And Pilate answered and said again unto them,

C: What will ye then that I shall do unto him whom ye call the King of the Jews?

N: And they cried out again,

C: Crucify him.

N: Then Pilate said unto them,

C: Why, what evil hath he done?

N: And they cried out the more exceedingly,

C: Crucify him.

N: And so Pilate, willing to content the people, released Barabbas unto them, and delivered Jesus, when he had scourged him, to be crucified. And the soldiers led him away into the hall, called Prætorium; and they call together the whole band. And they clothed him with purple, and platted a crown of thorns, and put it about his head, And began to salute him,

C: Hail, King of the Jews!

N: And they smote him on the head with a reed, and did spit upon him, and bowing their knees worshipped him. And when they had mocked him, they took off the purple from him, and put his own clothes on him, and led him out to crucify him. The rough-hewn wood of the lumberous cross splintered into the very muscles and sinews laid bare by the scourging. And they compel one Simon a Cyrenian, who passed by, coming out of the country, the father of Alexander and Rufus, to bear his stout cross. And there followed him a great company of people, and of women, which also bewailed and lamented him. But Jesus turning unto them said,

†: Daughters of Jerusalem, weep not for me, but weep for yourselves, and for your children. For, behold, the days are coming, in the which they shall say, Blessed are the barren, and the wombs that never bare, and the paps which never gave suck. Then shall they begin to say to the mountains, Fall on us; and to the hills, Cover us. For if they do these things in a green tree, what shall be done in the dry?

N: And they bring him unto the place Golgotha, which is, being interpreted, The place of a skull. And they gave him to drink wine mingled with myrrh: but he received it not. They laid Jesus upon the cross and stretched out his arms so his bones are out of joint, in accordance with the scriptures. The spikes were pounded into the wrists of his hands. With each hammer pain quaked through his body. The soliders hoisted up the cross with a shocking thud. And when they had crucified him, they parted his garments, casting lots upon them, what every man should take And it was the third hour, when they crucified him. And the superscription of his accusation was written over, THE KING OF THE JEWS. And with him they crucify two thieves; the one on his right hand, and the other on his left. And the scripture was fulfilled, which saith, And he was numbered with the transgressors And they that passed by railed on him, wagging their heads, and saying,

C: Ah, thou that destroyest the temple, and buildest it in three days, Save thyself, and come down from the cross.

N: Likewise also the chief priests mocking said among themselves with the scribes,

C: He saved others; himself he cannot save. Let Christ the King of Israel descend now from the cross, that we may see and believe.

N: And they that were crucified with him reviled him. And when the sixth hour was come, there was darkness over the whole land until the ninth hour. And at the ninth hour Jesus cried with a loud voice, saying,

†: Eloi, Eloi, lama sabachthani?

N: Which is, being interpreted, My God, my God, why hast thou forsaken me? And some of them that stood by, when they heard it, said,

C: Behold, he calleth Elias.

N: And one ran and filled a spunge full of vinegar, and put it on a reed, and gave him to drink, saying, Let alone; let us see whether Elias will come to take him down. And Jesus cried with a loud voice,

†: It is finished!

N: The Jews therefore, because it was the preparation,

C: The bodies should not remain upon the cross on the sabbath day, (for that sabbath day was an high day,) beseech Pilate that their legs might be broken, and that they might be taken away.

N: Then came the soldiers, and brake the legs of the first, and of the other which was crucified with him. But when they came to Jesus, and saw that he was dead already, they brake not his legs, in accordance with the scriptures. But one of the soldiers with a spear pierced his side, and forthwith came there out blood and water. And the veil of the temple was rent in twain from the top to the bottom. And when the centurion, which stood over against him, saw that he so cried out, and gave up the ghost, he said,

V: Truly this man was the Son of God.

N: There were also women looking on afar off: among whom was Mary Magdalene, and Mary the mother of James the less and of Joses, and Salome; (Who also, when he was in Galilee, followed him, and ministered unto him;) and many other women which came up with him unto Jerusalem. And now when the even was come, because it was the preparation, that is, the day before the sabbath, Joseph of Arimathæa, an honourable counseller, which also waited for the kingdom of God, came, and went in boldly unto Pilate, and craved the body of Jesus. And Pilate marvelled if he were already dead: and calling unto him the centurion, he asked him whether he had been any while dead. And when he knew it of the centurion, he gave the body to Joseph. The young man clothed in the linen cloth bathed the body of his Lord; he lamented,

V: The beauty of Israel is slain upon thy high places: how are the mighty fallen! Thy hands were pierced, and thy feet put upon the block: as a man falleth before wicked men, so fellest thou. And the young man wept again over him. Praise be to God! My Lord had not been buried with the burial of an ass, drawn and cast forth beyond the gates of Jerusalem; To given unto the ravenous birds of every sort, and to the beasts of the field to be devoured.

N: And the young man bought fine linen, and took him down, and wrapped him in the linen, and laid him in a sepulchre which was hewn out of a rock, and the stone was rolled unto the door of the sepulchre over them both. And it came to pass in the darkness, the young man lamented,

V: Shall the Lord of hosts not visit them for these things? shall not his soul be avenged on such a nation as this? For the mountains will he take up a weeping and wailing, and for the habitations of the wilderness a lamentation, because they are burned up, so that none can pass through them; neither can men hear the voice of the cattle; both the fowl of the heavens and the beast are fled; they are gone. And he will make Jerusalem heaps, and a den of dragons; and he will make the cities of Judah desolate, without an inhabitant. He will scatter them also among the heathen, whom neither they nor their fathers have known: and he will send a sword after them, till he hath consumed them.

N: And Mary Magdalene and Mary the mother of Joses beheld where he was laid. And that day was the preparation, and the sabbath drew on Jesus descended into Hades to preach the Gospel also to them that are dead, that they might be judged according to men in the flesh, but live according to God in the spirit. Thus he went in, and entered the foremost circle that surrounds the abyss and there were lamentations none, but only sighs, that tremble made the everlasting air. And this arose from sorrow without torment, which the crowds had, that many were and great of infants and of women and of men; That they sinned not; and if they merit had, 'tis not enough, because they had not baptism which is the portal of the Faith thou holdest; And if they were before Christ, in the right manner they

adored not God the Father and God the Son and God the Holy Ghost; For such defects, and not for other guilt, lost are they and are only so far punished, that without hope they live on in desire. Hence drew forth the shade of the First and that of his son Abel, and of Noah, of Moses the lawgiver; And the obedient Abraham, patriarch, and David, king, Israel with his father and his children, and Rachel, for whose sake he did so much; And others many, and he made them blessed; and thou must know, that earlier than these never were any human spirits saved. Jesus said unto the patriarchs,

†: But I would not have you to be ignorant, brethren, concerning ye which are asleep, that ye sorrow not, even as others which have no hope. For if ye believe that I died and will rise again, even so ye also which sleep in Jesus will God bring with him For this we say unto you by the word of the Lord, that we which are alive and remain unto the coming of the Lord shall not prevent them which are asleep. For I myself hath descended into Hades with a shout, with the voice of the archangel, and with the trump of God: and the dead in Christ shall rise first: Then ye which are dead and remain shall be caught up together with them in the depths, to meet the Lord in the depths: and so shall we ever be with the Lord. Wherefore comfort one another with these words.

N: And Satan said unto Jesus,

V: By Adam's sin hath I acquired dominion over his sons. Hath not God giveth me his Son as ransom? Shalt not I have dominion of death over Christ?

N: Jesus said,

†: Did I not behold Satan as lightning fall from heaven? Even the devils are subject unto my name. Forasmuch then as the children are partakers of flesh and blood, I also myself likewise took

part of the same; that through death I might destroy you that had the power of death, that is, the devil;And deliver them who through fear of death were all their lifetime subject to bondage.

N: To the patriarchs doth Jesus say,

†: The God of peace shall bruise Satan under your feet shortly. The grace of the Lord Jesus Christ be with you. Amen.

Harrowing Saturday

Apostles' Creed *(Said in the stead of The Dionicene Creed)*
Legion of CENOBITES

Mockest we their belief in God, the Father Almighty, Creator of heaven and earth; and in Jesus Christ, His only Son, their Lord: Who was conceived by the Holy Spirit, born of the Virgin Mary; suffered under Pontius Pilate, was crucified, died and was buried. He descended into hell; the third day He rose again from the dead; He ascended into heaven, is seated at the right hand of God the Father Almighty; from thence He shall come to judge the living and the dead. I believe in the Holy Spirit, the Holy Catholic Church, the communion of Saints, the forgiveness of sins, the resurrection of the body, and life everlasting. Amen.

Shemhamphorasch!

Collection *(Said after The Glory, but before the First Reading)*
HIGH-PRIEST

O God, ye signed a covenant with Satan, as god of this world, to giveth him dominion over your Son, Jesus the Christ. And as Jesus breaketh thy covenant with the national and people of Israel, ye hath broken thy covenant with thy most faithful servant and the prosecutor in thy court. Thy lieth with every breathe of silence. Thy covenants are nary worth a watery shit!

Legion of CENOBITES

Shemhamphorasch!

HIGH-PRIEST

O God, thy crimes are numerous. Satan shalt prosecute thee in the court of Heaven and thy shalt be found guilty of covenant breaking for Satan will even deal with thee as thou hast done, which hast despised the oath in breaking the covenant. Seeing ye despised the oath by breaking the covenant, when, lo, ye had given your hand, and hath done all these things, ye shall not escape.

The First Reading
HIGH-PRIEST

A reading from the book of Zechariah:

A Member of the CENOBITES

Rejoice greatly, O daughter of Zion; shout, O daughter of Jerusalem: behold, thy King cometh unto thee: he is just, and having salvation; lowly, and riding upon an ass, and upon a colt the foal of an ass. And I will cut off the chariot from Ephraim, and the horse from Jerusalem, and the battle bow shall be cut off: and he shall speak peace unto the heathen: and his dominion shall be from sea even to sea, and from the river even to the ends of the earth. As for thee also, by the blood of thy covenant I have sent forth thy prisoners out of the pit wherein is no water. Turn you to the strong hold, ye prisoners of hope: even to day do I declare that I will render double unto thee; When I have bent Judah for me, filled the bow with Ephraim, and raised up thy sons, O Zion, against thy sons, O Greece, and made thee as the sword of a mighty man. And the Lord shall be seen over them, and his arrow shall go forth as the lightning: and the Lord God shall blow the trumpet, and shall go with whirlwinds of the south. The Lord of hosts shall defend them; and they shall devour, and subdue with sling stones; and they shall drink, and make a noise as through wine; and they shall be filled like bowls, and as the corners of the altar. And the Lord their God shall save them in that day as the flock of his people: for they shall be as the stones of a crown, lifted up as an ensign upon his land. For how great is his goodness, and how great is his beauty! corn shall make the young men cheerful, and new wine the maids.

HIGH-PRIEST

The curs'd Word our enemy!

The Second Reading

HIGH-PRIEST

A reading from the First Epistle Peter:

A Member of the CENOBITES

And who is he that will harm you, if ye be followers of that which is good? But and if ye suffer for righteousness' sake, happy are ye: and be not afraid of their terror, neither be troubled; But sanctify the Lord God in your hearts: and be ready always to give an answer to every man that asketh you a reason of the hope that is in you with meekness and fear: Having a good conscience; that, whereas they speak evil of you, as of evildoers, they may be ashamed that falsely accuse your good conversation in Christ. For it is better, if the will of God be so, that ye suffer for well doing, than for evil doing. For Christ also hath once suffered for sins, the just for the unjust, that he might bring us to God, being put to death in the flesh, but quickened by the Spirit: By which also he went and preached unto the spirits in prison; Which sometime were disobedient, when once the longsuffering of God waited in the days of Noah, while the ark was a preparing, wherein few, that is, eight souls were saved by water. The like figure whereunto even baptism doth also now save us (not the putting away of the filth of the flesh, but the answer of a good conscience toward God,) by the resurrection of Jesus Christ: Who is gone into heaven, and is on the right hand of God; angels and authorities and powers being made subject unto him.

HIGH-PRIEST

The curs'd Word our enemy!

The Reading of the Gospel

HIGH-PRIEST

A reading from the Apocalypse according to John: And there was war in heaven: Michael and his angels fought against the dragon; and the dragon fought and his angels, And prevailed not; neither was their place found any more in heaven. And the great dragon was cast out, that old serpent, called the Devil, and Satan, which deceiveth the whole world: he was cast out into the earth, and his angels were cast out with him. And I heard a loud voice saying in heaven, Now is come salvation, and strength, and the kingdom of our God, and the power of his Christ: for the accuser of our brethren is cast down, which accused them before our God day and night. And they overcame him by the blood of the Lamb, and by the word of their testimony; and they loved not their lives unto the death. Therefore rejoice, ye heavens, and ye that dwell in them. Woe to the inhabiters of the earth and of the sea! for the devil is come down unto you, having great wrath, because he knoweth that he hath but a short time. And when the dragon saw that he was cast unto the earth, he persecuted the woman which brought forth the man child. And to the woman were given two wings of a great eagle, that she might fly into the wilderness, into her place, where she is nourished for a time, and times, and half a time, from the face of the serpent. And the serpent cast out of his mouth water as a flood after the woman, that he might cause her to be carried away of the flood. And the earth helped the woman, and the earth opened her mouth, and swallowed up the flood which the dragon cast out of his mouth. And the dragon was wroth with the woman, and went to make war with the remnant of her seed, which keep the commandments of God, and have the testimony of Jesus Christ.

Legion of CENOBITES

Curs'd be the Word of God.

HIGH-PRIEST

All glory to thee, O Satan. All praise
To thee, O Satan. May the curses of
This Gospel tattoos our sins upon
Our foreheads in the curs'd Mark of the Beast.

The Harrowing by Our Enemy!

N: NARRATOR V: VOICE
†: CHRIST C: CHORUS

N: The Harrowing by their Lord Jesus Christ! And Mary Magdalene and Mary the mother of Joses beheld where he was laid. God, the truest father of lies, signed a covenant with Satan, as rightful god of this world, giving him dominion over the Christ. When Jesus came upon the Baptist for His baptism, And it had come to pass in those days, that Jesus came from Nazareth of Galilee, and was baptized of John in Jordan. And straightway coming up out of the water, he saw the heavens opened, and the Spirit like a dove descending upon him: And there came a voice from heaven, saying,

V: Thou art my beloved Son, in whom I am well pleased.

N: And immediately the Spirit driveth him into the wilderness. And whilst he fasted forty days and forty nights, Satan ascended to the heights of heaven to present himself before the Lord. And the Lord said unto Satan,

V: Whence comest thou?

N: Then Satan answered the Lord, and said,

V: As god of their world, I crown their kings, shew signs to their priests, and murder their children, I rule over the living and the dead, tempting them all into sin. Rememberest when ye said unto me, Hast thou considered my creation man now apart from Eden, that there is no like him in the earth, a perfect and upright creation, one that feateth God and escheweth evil? Then

I answered ye, and said, Doth man fear God for nought? Hast not they been tempted of my temptations; hast not they learnt the knowledge of good and evil? hast not they delighteth in sin and debauchery as art and poetry? Hast not they murdered their brothers and banished their fathers and enslaved their sons; hast not they raped their mothers and burnt their sisters and maketh harlots of their daughters? Hast not they created of their own fancy gods and goddesses to pray to instead of thee; hast not they formed idols to worship instead of thee? But put forth thine hand now, and touch any that they have, and they will curse thee to thy face. Rememberest ye said unto me, Behold, all that man hath is in thy power; ye shall be god of their world; crown their kings, shew signs to their priests, and murder their children; rule over both the living and the dead, tempt them all into sin.

N: And the Lord said unto Satan,

V: I rememberest well.

N: And Satan said unto the Lord,

V: By Adam's sin hath I acquired dominion over his sons. Shalt ye giveth me thy Son as ransom? Shalt not I have dominion of death over Christ?

N: And the Lord said unto Satan,

V: Hast not thee met there my beloved Son, in whom I am well pleased, for there is none like him that has ever lived; For I so love the world that I shall give my only begotten Son, that whosoever believeth in him should not perish, but have eternal life. For I sendeth not my Son into the world to condemn the world; but that the world through him might be saved.

N: Then Satan answered the Lord, and said,

V: Doth thy begotten Son understand the true nature of sin? Hast he known sin who is made to be sin for man? Hast he committed any sin; hast any deception be found in his mouth? And the Lord said unto Satan, None.But put forth thine hand now, and touch all that he hath, and he will curse you!

N: And the Lord said unto Satan,

V: Behold, all that he hath is in thy power; only upon himself put not forth thine hand until the time has come; I shalt giveth thee my Son as ransom to emancipate the sons of Adam for that original sin; and I shalt giveth thee dominion of death over Christ, my only Begotten Son! Tempt his enemies into murdering him; tempt his friends into betraying him; tempt him with every temptation ye hast ever tempted man with.

N: And Jesus was there in the wilderness forty days, tempted of Satan; and was with the wild beasts; and the angels ministered unto him. The Lord saith,

V: My Son, my Son, ye shalt never forsake me!

N: And on that day which was the preparation, Satan prepared to accept dominion over Jesus, and when the sabbath drew on Jesus descended into Hades to preach the Gospel also to them that are dead, that they might be judged according to men in the flesh, but live according to God in the spirit.

V: Thus he went in, and entered the foremost circle that surrounds the abyss and there were lamentations none, but only sighs, that tremble made the everlasting air. And this arose from sorrow without torment, which the crowds had, that many were and great of infants and of women and of men; That they sinned not; and if they merit had, 'tis not enough, because they had not baptism which is the portal of the Faith thou holdest; And if they were before Christ, in the right manner they adored not God the Father and God the Son and God the Holy Ghost; For such defects, and not for other guilt, lost are they and are only so far punished, that without hope they live on in desire. Hence drew forth the shade of the First and that of his son Abel, and of Noah, of Moses the lawgiver;And the obedient Abraham, patriarch, and David, king, Israel with his father and his children, and Rachel, for whose sake he did so much; And others many, and he made them blessed; and thou must know, that earlier than these never were any human spirits saved. Jesus said unto the patriarchs:

†: But I would not have you to be ignorant, brethren, concerning ye which are asleep, that ye sorrow not, even as others which have no hope. For if ye believe that I died and will rise again, even so ye also which sleep in Jesus will God bring with him. For this we say unto you by the word of the Lord, that we which are alive and remain unto the coming of the Lord shall not prevent them which are asleep. For I myself hath descended into Hades with a shout, with the voice of the archangel, and with the trump of God: and the dead in Christ shall rise first: Then ye which are dead and remain shall be caught up together with them in the depths, to meet the Lord in the depths: and so shall we ever be with the Lord. Wherefore comfort one another with these words.

V: And Satan said unto Jesus, By Adam's sin hath I acquired dominion over his sons. Hath not God giveth me his Son as ransom? Shalt not I have dominion of death over Christ? Jesus said,

†: Did I not behold Satan as lightning fall from heaven? Even the devils are subject unto my name. Forasmuch then as the children are partakers of flesh and blood, I also myself likewise took part of the same; that through death I might destroy you that had the power of death, that is, the devil; And deliver them who through fear of death were all their lifetime subject to bondage.

V: To the patriarchs doth Jesus say,

†: The God of peace shall bruise Satan under your feet shortly. The grace of the Lord Jesus Christ be with you. Amen.

Easter Sunday
The First Reading

Hɪɢʜ-Pʀɪᴇsᴛ

A reading from the Acts of the Apostles:

A Member of the Cᴇɴᴏʙɪᴛᴇs

Then Peter opened his mouth, and said, Ye know, which was published throughout all Judaea, and began from Galilee, after the baptism which John preached; How God anointed Jesus of Nazareth with the Holy Ghost and with power: who went about doing good, and healing all that were oppressed of the devil; for God was with him. And we are witnesses of all things which he did both in the land of the Jews, and in Je-rusalem; whom they slew and hanged on a tree: Him God raised up the third day, and shewed him openly; Not to all the people, but unto witnesses chosen before God, even to us, who did eat and drink with him after he rose from the dead. And he commanded us to preach unto the people, and to testify that it is he which was ordained of God to be the Judge of quick and dead. To him give all the prophets witness, that through his name whosoever believeth in him shall receive remission of sins.

Hɪɢʜ-Pʀɪᴇsᴛ

The curs'd Word our enemy!

The Second Reading

Hɪɢʜ-Pʀɪᴇsᴛ

A reading from the First Epistle Peter:

A Member of the Cᴇɴᴏʙɪᴛᴇs

Know ye not that a little leaven leaveneth the whole lump? Purge out therefore the old leaven, that ye may be a new lump, as ye are unleavened. For even Christ our passover is sacrificed for us: Therefore let us keep the feast, not with old leaven, neither with the leaven of malice and wickedness; but with the unleavened bread of sincerity and truth. I wrote unto you in an epistle not to company with fornicators: Yet not altogether with the fornicators of this world, or with the covetous, or extortioners, or with idolaters; for then must ye needs go out of the world. But now I have written unto you not to keep company, if any man that is called a brother be a fornicator, or covetous, or an idolator, or a railer, or a drunkard, or an extortioner; with such an one no not to eat. For what have I to do to judge them also that are without? do not ye judge them that are within? But them that are without God judgeth. Therefore put away from among yourselves that wicked person.

Hɪɢʜ-Pʀɪᴇsᴛ

The curs'd Word our enemy!

The Reading of the Gospel

HIGH-PRIEST

A reading from the Gospel of Matthew: Now the next day, that followed the day of the preparation, the chief priests and Pharisees came together unto Pilate, Saying, Sir, we remember that that deceiver said, while he was yet alive, After three days I will rise again. Command therefore that the sepulchre be made sure until the third day, lest his disciples come by night, and steal him away, and say unto the people, He is risen from the dead: so the last error shall be worse than the first. Pilate said unto them, Ye have a watch: go your way, make it as sure as ye can. So they went, and made the sepulchre sure, sealing the stone, and setting a watch. In the end of the sabbath, as it began to dawn toward the first day of the week, came Mary Magdalene and the other Mary to see the sepulchre. And, behold, there was a great earthquake: for the angel of the Lord descended from heaven, and came and rolled back the stone from the door, and sat upon it. His countenance was like lightning, and his raiment white as snow: And for fear of him the keepers did shake, and became as dead men. And the angel answered and said unto the women, Fear not ye: for I know that ye seek Jesus, which was crucified. He is not here: for he is risen, as he said. Come, see the place where the Lord lay. And go quickly, and tell his disciples that he is risen from the dead; and, behold, he goeth before you into Galilee; there shall ye see him: lo, I have told you. Now when they were going, behold, some of the watch came into the city, and shewed unto the chief priests all the things that were done. And when they were assembled with the elders, and had taken counsel, they gave large money unto the soldiers, Saying, Say ye, His disciples came by night, and stole him away while we slept. And if this come to the governor's ears, we will persuade him, and secure you. So they took the money, and did as they were taught: and this saying is commonly reported among the Jews until this day.

Legion of CENOBITES

Curs'd be the Word of God.

HIGH-PRIEST

All glory to thee, O Satan. All praise
To thee, O Satan. May the curses of
This Gospel tattoos our sins upon
Our foreheads in the curs'd Mark of the Beast.

Pentecost

The First Reading

HIGH-PRIEST

A reading from the Acts of the Apostles:

A Member of the CENOBITES

And when the day of Pentecost was fully come, they were all with one accord in one place. And suddenly there came a sound from heaven as of a rushing mighty wind, and it filled all the house where they were sitting. And there appeared unto them cloven tongues like as of fire, and it sat upon each of them. And they were all filled with the Holy Ghost, and began to speak with other tongues, as the Spirit gave them utterance. And there were dwelling at Jerusalem Jews, devout men, out of every nation under heaven. Now when this was noised abroad, the multitude came together, and were confounded, because that every man heard them speak in his own language. And they were all amazed and marvelled, saying one to another, Behold, are not all these which speak Galilaeans? And how hear we every man in our own tongue, wherein we were born? Parthians, and Medes, and Elamites, and the dwellers in Mesopotamia, and in Judaea, and Cappadocia, in Pontus and Asia, Phrygia, and Pamphylia, in Egypt, and in the parts of Libya about Cyrene, and strangers of Rome, Jews and proselytes, Cretes and Arabians, we do hear them speak in our tongues the wonderful works of God.

HIGH-PRIEST

The curs'd Word our enemy!

The Second Reading

HIGH-PRIEST

A reading from the First Epistle Peter:

A Member of the CENOBITES

Brothers and sisters: No man can say that Jesus is the Lord, but by the Holy Ghost. Now there are diversities of gifts, but the same Spirit. And there are differences of administrations, but the same Lord. And there are diversities of operations, but it is the same God which worketh all in all. But the manifestation of the Spirit is given to every man to profit withal. For as the body is one, and hath many members, and all the members of that one body, being many, are one body: so also is Christ. For by one Spirit are we all baptized into one body, whether we be Jews or Gentiles, whether we be bond or free; and have been all made to drink into one Spirit.

HIGH-PRIEST

The curs'd Word our enemy!

The Reading of the Gospel

HIGH-PRIEST

A reading from the Gospel of John: Then the same day at evening, being the first day of the week, when the doors were shut where the disciples were assembled for fear of the Jews, came Jesus and stood in the midst, and saith unto them, Peace be unto you. And when he had so said, he shewed unto them his hands and his side. Then were the disciples glad, when they saw the Lord. Then said Jesus to them again, Peace be unto you: as my Father hath sent me, even so send I you. And when he had said this, he breathed on them, and saith unto them, Receive ye the Holy Ghost: Whose soever sins ye remit, they are remitted unto them; and whose soever sins ye retain, they are retained.

Legion of CENOBITES

Curs'd be the Word of God.

HIGH-PRIEST

All glory to thee, O Satan. All praise
To thee, O Satan. May the curses of
This Gospel tattoos our sins upon
Our foreheads in the curs'd Mark of the Beast.

Readings on Fornication

The First Reading

HIGH-PRIEST

A reading from the book of Leviticus:

A Member of the CENOBITES

None of you shall approach to any that is near of kin to him, to uncover their nakedness: I am the LORD. The nakedness of thy father, or the nakedness of thy mother, shalt thou not uncover: she is thy mother; thou shalt not uncover her nakedness. The nakedness of thy father's wife shalt thou not uncover: it is thy father's nakedness. The nakedness of thy sister, the daughter of thy father, or daughter of thy mother, whether she be born at home, or born abroad, even their nakedness thou shalt not uncover. The nakedness of thy son's daughter, or of thy daughter's daughter, even their nakedness thou shalt not uncover: for theirs is thine own nakedness. The nakedness of thy father's wife's daughter, begotten of thy father, she is thy sister, thou shalt not uncover her nakedness. Thou shalt not uncover the nakedness of thy father's sister: she is thy father's near kinswoman. Thou shalt not uncover the nakedness of thy mother's sister: for she is thy mother's near kinswoman. Thou shalt not uncover the nakedness of thy father's brother, thou shalt not approach to his wife: she is thine aunt. Thou shalt not uncover the nakedness of thy daughter in law: she is thy son's wife; thou shalt not uncover her nakedness. Thou shalt not uncover the nakedness of thy brother's wife: it is thy brother's nakedness. Thou shalt not uncover the nakedness of a woman and her daughter, neither shalt thou take her son's daughter, or her daughter's daughter, to uncover her nakedness; for they are her near kinswomen: it is wickedness. Neither shalt thou take a wife to her sister, to vex her, to uncover her nakedness, beside the other in her life time. Also thou shalt not approach unto a woman to uncover her nakedness, as long as she is put apart for her uncleanness. Moreover thou shalt not lie carnally with thy neighbour's wife, to defile thyself with her. And thou shalt not let any of thy seed pass through the fire to Molech, neither shalt thou profane the name of thy God: I am the LORD. Thou shalt not lie with mankind, as with womankind: it is abomination. Neither shalt thou lie with any beast to defile thyself therewith: neither shall any woman stand before a beast to lie down thereto: it is confusion. Defile not ye yourselves in any of these things: for in all these the nations are defiled which I cast out before you: And the land is defiled: therefore I do visit the iniquity thereof upon it, and the land itself vomiteth out her inhabitants. Ye shall therefore keep my statutes and my judgments, and shall not commit any of these abominations; neither any of your own nation, nor any stranger that sojourneth among you: (For all these abominations have the men of the land done, which were before you, and the land is defiled;) that the land spue not you out also, when ye defile it, as it spued out the nations that were before you. For whosoever shall commit any of these abominations, even the souls that commit them shall be cut off from among their people. Therefore shall ye keep mine ordinance, that ye commit not any one of these abominable customs, which were committed before you, and that ye defile not yourselves therein: I am the LORD your God.

High-Priest

The curs'd Word our enemy!

The Second Reading

High-Priest

A reading from the first epistle of Paul to the Corinthians:

A Member of the Cenobites

DARE any of you, having a matter against another, go to law before the unjust, and not before the saints? Do ye not know that the saints shall judge the world? and if the world shall be judged by you, are ye unworthy to judge the smallest matters? Know ye not that we shall judge angels? how much more things that pertain to this life? If then ye have judgments of things pertaining to this life, set them to judge who are least esteemed in the church. I speak to your shame. Is it so, that there is not a wise man among you? no, not one that shall be able to judge between his brethren? But brother goeth to law with brother, and that before the unbelievers. Now therefore there is utterly a fault among you, because ye go to law one with another. Why do ye not rather take wrong? why do ye not rather suffer yourselves to be defrauded? Nay, ye do wrong, and defraud, and that your brethren. Know ye not that the unrighteous shall not inherit the kingdom of God? Be not deceived: neither fornicators, nor idolaters, nor adulterers, nor effeminate, nor abusers of themselves with mankind, Nor thieves, nor covetous, nor drunkards, nor revilers, nor extortioners, shall inherit the kingdom of God. And such were some of you: but ye are washed, but ye are sanctified, but ye are justified in the name of the Lord Jesus, and by the Spirit of our God. All things are lawful unto me, but all things are not expedient: all things are lawful for me, but I will not be brought under the power of any. Meats for the belly, and the belly for meats: but God shall destroy both it and them. Now the body is not for fornication, but for the Lord; and the Lord for the body. And God hath both raised up the Lord, and will also raise up us by his own power. Know ye not that your bodies are the members of Christ? shall I then take the members of Christ, and make them the members of an harlot? God forbid. What? know ye not that he which is joined to an harlot is one body? for two, saith he, shall be one flesh. But he that is joined unto the Lord is one spirit. Flee fornication. Every sin that a man doeth is without the body; but he that committeth fornication sinneth against his own body. What? know ye not that your body is the temple of the Holy Ghost which is in you, which ye have of God, and ye are not your own? For ye are bought with a price: therefore glorify God in your body, and in your spirit, which are God's.

High-Priest

The curs'd Word our enemy!

The Reading of the Gospel

High-Priest

A reading from the Secret Gospel according to Mark: And they were in the way going up to Jerusalem; and Jesus went before them: and they were amazed; and as they followed, they were afraid. And he took again the twelve, and began to tell them what things should happen unto him, Saying, Behold, we go up to Jerusalem; and the Son of man shall be delivered unto the chief priests, and unto the scribes; and they shall condemn him to death, and shall deliver him to the Gentiles: And they shall mock him, and shall scourge him, and shall spit upon him, and shall kill him: and the third day he shall rise again. And they come into Bethany. And a certain woman whose brother had died was there. And, coming, she prostrated herself before Jesus and says to him, 'Son of David, have mercy on me.' But the disciples rebuked her. And Jesus, being angered, went off with her into the garden where the tomb was, and straightway a great cry was heard from the tomb. And going near, Jesus rolled away the stone from the door of the tomb. And straightaway, going in where the youth was, he stretched forth his hand and raised him, seizing his hand. But the youth, looking upon Him, *loved Him* and began to beseech Him that *he might be with Him.* And going out of the tomb, they came into the house of the youth, for he was rich. And after six days Jesus told him what to do, and in the evening the youth comes to him, wearing a linen cloth over his naked body. And he remained with him that night, for Jesus taught him the mystery of the Kingdom of God. And thence, arising, he returned to the other side of the Jordan... And there followed him a certain young man, having a linen cloth cast about his naked body; and the young men laid hold on him: And he left the linen cloth, and fled from them naked... And whenst they wouldst look at Jesus' tomb, they saw that the stone was rolled away: for it was very great. And entering into the sepulchre, they saw a young man sitting on the right side, clothed in a long white garment; and they were affrighted.

Legion of CENOBITES

Curs'd be the Word of God.

HIGH-PRIEST

All glory to thee, O Satan. All praise
To thee, O Satan. May the curses of
This Gospel tattoos our sins upon
Our foreheads in the curs'd Mark of the Beast.

Readings on Exorcism
The First Reading

HIGH-PRIEST

A reading from the Testament of Solomon:

A Member of the CENOBITES

And Solomon commanded another demon to come before him. And there came before his face thirty-six spirits, their heads shapeless like dogs, but in themselves they were human in form; with faces of asses, faces of oxen, and faces of birds. And Solomon, on hearing and seeing them, wondered, and he asked them and said: Who are you? But they, of one accord with one voice, said: We are the thirty-six elements, the world-rulers of this darkness. But, O King Solomon, thou wilt not wrong us nor imprison us, nor lay command on us; but since the Lord God has given thee authority over every spirit, in the air, and on the earth, and under the earth, therefore do we also present ourselves before thee like the other spirits, from ram and bull, from both twin and crab, lion and virgin, scales and scorpion, archer, goat-horned, water-pourer, and fish. Then Solomon invoked the name of the Lord Sabaoth, and questioned each in turn as to what was its character. And he bade each one come forward and tell of its actions.... And Solomon, when he heard this, glorified the God of heaven and earth. And he commanded them to fetch water in the Temple of God. And he furthermore prayed to the Lord God to cause the demons without, that hamper humanity, to be bound and made to approach the Temple of God. Some of these demons he condemned to do the heavy work of the construction of the Temple of God. Others he shut up in prisons. Others he ordered to wrestle with fire in (the making of) gold and silver, sitting down by lead and spoon. And to make ready places for the other demons in which they should be confined.

HIGH-PRIEST

The curs'd Word our enemy!

The Second Reading

HIGH-PRIEST

A reading from the epistle of Paul to the Corinthians:

A Member of the CENOBITES

speak as to wise men; judge ye what I say. The cup of blessing which we bless, is it not the communion of the blood of Christ? The bread which we break, is it not the communion of the body of Christ? For we being many are one bread, and one body: for we are all partakers of that one bread. Behold Israel after the flesh: are not they which eat of the sacrifices partakers of the altar? What say I then? that the idol is any thing, or that which is offered in sacrifice to idols is any thing? But I say, that the things which the Gentiles sacrifice, they sacrifice to devils, and not to God: and I would not that ye should have fellowship with devils. Ye cannot drink the cup of the

Lord, and the cup of devils: ye cannot be partakers of the Lord's table, and of the table of devils. Do we provoke the Lord to jealousy? are we stronger than he? Be ye not unequally yoked together with unbelievers: for what fellowship hath righteousness with unrighteousness? and what communion hath light with darkness? And what concord hath Christ with Belial? or what part hath he that believeth with an infidel? And what agreement hath the temple of God with idols? for ye are the temple of the living God; as God hath said, I will dwell in them, and walk in them; and I will be their God, and they shall be my people. Wherefore come out from among them, and be ye separate, saith the Lord, and touch not the unclean thing; and I will receive you, And will be a Father unto you, and ye shall be my sons and daughters, saith the Lord Almighty. Let not sin therefore reign in your mortal body, that ye should obey it in the lusts thereof. Neither yield ye your members as instruments of unrighteousness unto sin: but yield yourselves unto God, as those that are alive from the dead, and your members as instruments of righteousness unto God. For sin shall not have dominion over you: for ye are not under the law, but under grace.

HIGH-PRIEST

The curs'd Word our enemy!

The Reading of the Gospel

HIGH-PRIEST

A reading from the Curs'd Gospel according to Matthew: Then was brought unto him one possessed with a devil, blind, and dumb: and he healed him, insomuch that the blind and dumb both spake and saw. And all the people were amazed, and said, Is not this the son of David? But when the Pharisees heard it, they said, This fellow doth not cast out devils, but by Beelzebub the prince of the devils. And Jesus knew their thoughts, and said unto them, Every kingdom divided against itself is brought to desolation; and every city or house divided against itself shall not stand: And if Satan cast out Satan, he is divided against himself; how shall then his kingdom stand? And if I by Beelzebub cast out devils, by whom do your children cast them out? therefore they shall be your judges. But if I cast out devils by the Spirit of God, then the kingdom of God is come unto you. Or else how can one enter into a strong man's house, and spoil his goods, except he first bind the strong man? and then he will spoil his house. He that is not with me is against me; and he that gathereth not with me scattereth abroad. Wherefore I say unto you, All manner of sin and blasphemy shall be forgiven unto men: but the blasphemy against the Holy Ghost shall not be forgiven unto men. And whosoever speaketh a word against the Son of man, it shall be forgiven him: but whosoever speaketh against the Holy Ghost, it shall not be forgiven him, neither in this world, neither in the world to come. Either make the tree good, and his fruit good; or else make the tree corrupt, and his fruit corrupt: for the tree is known by his fruit. The queen of the south shall rise up in the judgment with this generation, and shall condemn it: for she came from the uttermost parts of the earth to hear the wisdom of Solomon; and, behold, a greater than Solomon is here.

Legion of CENOBITES

Curs'd be the Word of God.

HIGH-PRIEST

All glory to thee, O Satan. All praise
To thee, O Satan. May the curses of
This Gospel tattoos our sins upon
Our foreheads in the curs'd Mark of the Beast.

Readings on *Idolatry* & *Graven Imagery*

The First Reading

HIGH-PRIEST

A reading from the Book of Exodus:

A Member of the CENOBITES

And when the people saw that Moses delayed to come down out of the mount, the people gathered themselves together unto Aaron, and said unto him, Up, make us gods, which shall go before us; for as for this Moses, the man that brought us up out of the land of Egypt, we wot not what is become of him. And Aaron said unto them, Break off the golden earrings, which are in the ears of your wives, of your sons, and of your daughters, and bring them unto me. And all the people brake off the golden earrings which were in their ears, and brought them unto Aaron. And he received them at their hand, and fashioned it with a graving tool, after he had made it a molten calf: and they said, These be thy gods, O Israel, which brought thee up out of the land of Egypt. And when Aaron saw it, he built an altar before it; and Aaron made proclamation, and said, To morrow is a feast to the Lord. And they rose up early on the morrow, and offered burnt offerings, and brought peace offerings; and the people sat down to eat and to drink, and rose up to play. And the Lord said unto Moses, Go, get thee down; for thy people, which thou broughtest out of the land of Egypt, have corrupted themselves: They have turned aside quickly out of the way which I commanded them: they have made them a molten calf, and have worshipped it, and have sacrificed thereunto, and said, These be thy gods, O Israel, which have brought thee up out of the land of Egypt. And the Lord said unto Moses, I have seen this people, and, behold, it is a stiffnecked people: Now therefore let me alone, that my wrath may wax hot against them, and that I may consume them: and I will make of thee a great nation.

HIGH-PRIEST

The curs'd Word our enemy!

The Second Reading

HIGH-PRIEST

A reading from the second epistle of Paul to the Corinthians:

A Member of the CENOBITES

Wherefore, my dearly beloved, flee from idolatry. I speak as to wise men; judge ye what I say. The cup of blessing which we bless, is it not the communion of the blood of Christ? The bread which we break, is it not the communion of the body of Christ? For we being many are one bread, and one body: for we are all partakers of that one bread. Behold Israel after the flesh: are not they which eat of the sacrifices partakers of the altar? What say I then? that the idol is any thing, or that which is offered in sacrifice to idols is any thing? But I say, that the things which the Gentiles sacrifice, they sacrifice to devils, and not to God: and I would not that ye should have fellowship with devils. Ye cannot drink the cup of the Lord, and the cup of devils: ye cannot be partakers of the Lord's table, and of the table of devils.

High-Priest

The curs'd Word our enemy!

The Reading of the Gospel

High-Priest

A reading from the Curs'd Gospel according to John: And therefore did the Jews persecute Jesus, and sought to slay him, because he had done these things on the sabbath day. But Jesus answered them, My Father worketh hitherto, and I work. Therefore the Jews sought the more to kill him, because he not only had broken the sabbath, but said also that God was his Father, making himself equal with God. Then answered Jesus and said unto them, Verily, verily, I say unto you, The Son can do nothing of himself, but what he seeth the Father do: for what things soever he doeth, these also doeth the Son likewise. For the Father loveth the Son, and sheweth him all things that himself doeth: and he will shew him greater works than these, that ye may marvel. For as the Father raiseth up the dead, and quickeneth them; even so the Son quickeneth whom he will. For the Father judgeth no man, but hath committed all judgment unto the Son: That all men should honour the Son, even as they honour the Father. He that honoureth not the Son honoureth not the Father which hath sent him. Verily, verily, I say unto you, He that heareth my word, and believeth on him that sent me, hath everlasting life, and shall not come into condemnation; but is passed from death unto life. Verily, verily, I say unto you, The hour is coming, and now is, when the dead shall hear the voice of the Son of God: and they that hear shall live. For as the Father hath life in himself; so hath he given to the Son to have life in himself; And hath given him authority to execute judgment also, because he is the Son of man.

Legion of Cenobites

Curs'd be the Word of God.

High-Priest

All glory to thee, O Satan. All praise
To thee, O Satan. May the curses of
This Gospel tattoos our sins upon
Our foreheads in the curs'd Mark of the Beast.

Readings on Sabbath Breaking

The First Reading

HIGH-PRIEST

A reading from the Book of Prophet Ezekiel:

A *Member of the* CENOBITES

But the house of Israel rebelled against me in the wilderness: they walked not in my statutes, and they despised my judgments, which if a man do, he shall even live in them; and my sabbaths they greatly polluted: then I said, I would pour out my fury upon them in the wilderness, to consume them. But I wrought for my name's sake, that it should not be polluted before the heathen, in whose sight I brought them out. Yet also I lifted up my hand unto them in the wilderness, that I would not bring them into the land which I had given them, flowing with milk and honey, which is the glory of all lands; Because they despised my judgments, and walked not in my statutes, but polluted my sabbaths: for their heart went after their idols. Nevertheless mine eye spared them from destroying them, neither did I make an end of them in the wilderness. But I said unto their children in the wilderness, Walk ye not in the statutes of your fathers, neither observe their judgments, nor defile yourselves with their idols: I am the Lord your God; walk in my statutes, and keep my judgments, and do them; And hallow my sabbaths; and they shall be a sign between me and you, that ye may know that I am the Lord your God. Notwithstanding the children rebelled against me: they walked not in my statutes, neither kept my judgments to do them, which if a man do, he shall even live in them; they polluted my sabbaths: then I said, I would pour out my fury upon them, to accomplish my anger against them in the wilderness. Nevertheless I withdrew mine hand, and wrought for my name's sake, that it should not be polluted in the sight of the heathen, in whose sight I brought them forth. I lifted up mine hand unto them also in the wilderness, that I would scatter them among the heathen, and disperse them through the countries; Because they had not executed my judgments, but had despised my statutes, and had polluted my sabbaths, and their eyes were after their fathers' idols.

HIGH-PRIEST

The curs'd Word our enemy!

The Second Reading

HIGH-PRIEST

A reading from the epistle of Paul to the Colossians:

A *Member of the* CENOBITES

And you, being dead in your sins and the uncircumcision of your flesh, hath he quickened together with him, having forgiven you all trespasses; Blotting out the handwriting of ordinances that was against us, which was contrary to us, and took it out of the way, nailing it to his cross; And having spoiled principalities and powers, he made a shew of them openly, triumphing over them in it. Let no man therefore judge you in meat, or in drink, or in respect of an holyday, or of the new moon, or of the sabbath days: Which are a shadow of things to come; but the body is of Christ.

HIGH-PRIEST

The curs'd Word our enemy!

The Reading of the Gospel

HIGH-PRIEST

A reading from the Curs'd Gospel according to Mark: And it came to pass, that he went through the corn fields on the sabbath day; and his disciples began, as they went, to pluck the ears of corn. And the Pharisees said unto him, Behold, why do they on the sabbath day that which is not lawful? And he said unto them, Have ye never read what David did, when he had need, and was an hungred, he, and they that were with him? How he went into the house of God in the days of Abiathar the high priest, and did eat the shewbread, which is not lawful to eat but for the priests, and gave also to them which were with him? And he said unto them, The sabbath was made for man, and not man for the sabbath: Therefore the Son of man is Lord also of the sabbath. And he entered again into the synagogue; and there was a man there which had a withered hand. And they watched him, whether he would heal him on the sabbath day; that they might accuse him. And he saith unto the man which had the withered hand, Stand forth. And he saith unto them, Is it lawful to do good on the sabbath days, or to do evil? to save life, or to kill? But they held their peace. And when he had looked round about on them with anger, being grieved for the hardness of their hearts, he saith unto the man, Stretch forth thine hand. And he stretched it out: and his hand was restored whole as the other. And the Pharisees went forth, and straightway took counsel with the Herodians against him, how they might destroy him.

Legion of CENOBITES

Curs'd be the Word of God.

HIGH-PRIEST

All glory to thee, O Satan. All praise
To thee, O Satan. May the curses of
This Gospel tattoos our sins upon
Our foreheads in the curs'd Mark of the Beast.

Readings on Honouring Parents

The First Reading

High-Priest

A reading from the Book of Prophet Malachi:

A Member of the Cenobites

A son honoureth his father, and a servant his master: if then I be a father, where is mine honour? and if I be a master, where is my fear? saith the Lord of hosts unto you, O priests, that despise my name. And ye say, Wherein have we despised thy name? Ye offer polluted bread upon mine altar; and ye say, Wherein have we polluted thee? In that ye say, The table of the Lord is contemptible. And if ye offer the blind for sacrifice, is it not evil? and if ye offer the lame and sick, is it not evil? offer it now unto thy governor; will he be pleased with thee, or accept thy person? saith the Lord of hosts. But ye have profaned it, in that ye say, The table of the Lord is polluted; and the fruit thereof, even his meat, is contemptible. But cursed be the deceiver, which hath in his flock a male, and voweth, and sacrificeth unto the Lord a corrupt thing: for I am a great

King, saith the Lord of hosts, and my name is dreadful among the heathen.

High-Priest

The curs'd Word our enemy!

The Second Reading

High-Priest

A reading from the epistle of Paul to the Ephesians:

A Member of the Cenobites

Children, obey your parents in the Lord: for this is right. Honour thy father and mother; which is the first commandment with promise; That it may be well with thee, and thou mayest live long on the earth. And, ye fathers, provoke not your children to wrath: but bring them up in the nurture and admonition of the Lord. Servants, be obedient to them that are your masters according to the flesh, with fear and trembling, in singleness of your heart, as unto Christ; Not with eyeservice, as menpleasers; but as the servants of Christ, doing the will of God from the heart; With good will doing service, as to the Lord, and not to men: Knowing that whatsoever good thing any man doeth, the same shall he receive of the Lord, whether he be bond or free. And, ye masters, do the same things unto them, forbearing threatening: knowing that your Master also is in heaven; neither is there respect of persons with him.

High-Priest

The curs'd Word our enemy!

The Reading of the Gospel

HIGH-PRIEST

A reading from the Curs'd Gospel according to Mark: There came then his brethren and his mother, and, standing without, sent unto him, calling him. And the multitude sat about him, and they said unto him, Behold, thy mother and thy brethren without seek for thee. And he answered them, saying, Who is my mother, or my brethren? And he looked round about on them which sat about him, and said, Behold my mother and my brethren! For whosoever shall do the will of God, the same is my brother, and my sister, and mother. Verily, verily, I say unto thee, Except a man be born again, he cannot see the kingdom of God. And the multitude saith unto him, How can a man be born when he is old? can he enter the second time into his mother's womb, and be born? us answered, Verily, verily, I say unto thee, Except a man be born of water and of the Spirit, he cannot enter into the kingdom of God. That which is born of the flesh is flesh; and that which is born of the Spirit is spirit. Marvel not that I said unto thee, Ye must be born again. I rebuke the unsoiled gash out of I slimed!

Legion of CENOBITES

Curs'd be the Word of God.

HIGH-PRIEST

All glory to thee, O Satan. All praise
To thee, O Satan. May the curses of
This Gospel tattoos our sins upon
Our foreheads in the curs'd Mark of the Beast.

Readings on Murder

The First Reading

HIGH-PRIEST

A reading from the Book of Numbers:

A Member of the CENOBITES

But all the congregation bade stone them with stones. And the glory of the Lord appeared in the tabernacle of the congregation before all the children of Israel. And the Lord said unto Moses, How long will this people provoke me? and how long will it be ere they believe me, for all the signs which I have shewed among them? I will smite them with the pestilence, and disinherit them, and will make of thee a greater nation and mightier than they. And Moses said unto the Lord, Then the Egyptians shall hear it, (for thou broughtest up this people in thy might from among them;) And they will tell it to the inhabitants of this land: for they have heard that thou Lord art among this people, that thou Lord art seen face to face, and that thy cloud standeth over them, and that thou goest before them, by day time in a pillar of a cloud, and in a pillar of fire by night. Now if thou shalt kill all this people as one man, then the nations which have heard the fame of thee will speak, saying, Because the Lord was not able to bring this people into the land which he sware unto them, therefore he hath slain them in the wilderness.

HIGH-PRIEST

The curs'd Word our enemy!

The Second Reading

HIGH-PRIEST

A reading from the first epistle of Paul to the Corinthians:

A Member of the CENOBITES

Now this I say, that every one of you saith, I am of Paul; and I of Apollos; and I of Cephas; and I of Christ. Is Christ divided? was Paul crucified for you? or were ye baptized in the name of Paul? For the preaching of the cross is to them that perish foolishness; but unto us which are saved it is the power of God. For it is written, I will destroy the wisdom of the wise, and will bring to nothing the understanding of the prudent. Where is the wise? where is the scribe? where is the disputer of this world? hath not God made foolish the wisdom of this world? For after that in the wisdom of God the world by wisdom knew not God, it pleased God by the foolishness of preaching to save them that believe. For the Jews require a sign, and the Greeks seek after wisdom: But we preach Christ crucified, unto the Jews a stumblingblock, and unto the Greeks foolishness; But unto them which are called, both Jews and Greeks, Christ the power of God, and the wisdom of God. Because the foolishness of God is wiser than men; and the weakness of God is stronger than men.

HIGH-PRIEST

The curs'd Word our enemy!

The Reading of the Gospel

HIGH-PRIEST

A reading from the Curs'd Gospel according all of them fuckers: And the Pharisees went forth, and straightway took counsel with the Herodians against him, how they might destroy him. Therefore the Jews sought the more to kill him, because he not only had broken the sabbath, but said also that God was his Father, making himself equal with God. After these things Jesus walked in Galilee: for he would not walk in Jewry, because the Jews sought to kill him. But the chief priests consulted that they might put Lazarus also to death; sfter two days was the feast of the passover, and of unleavened bread: and the chief priests and the scribes sought how they might take him by craft, and put him to death. Then assembled together the chief priests, and the scribes, and the elders of the people, unto the palace of the high priest, who was called Caiaphas, And consulted that they might take Jesus by subtilty, and kill him. But Pilate answered them, saying, Will ye that I release unto you the King of the Jews? For he knew that the chief priests had delivered him for envy. But the chief priests and scribes sought how they might kill him; for they feared the people. But the chief priests moved the people, that he should rather release Barabbas unto them. And Pilate answered and said again unto them, What will ye then that I shall do unto him whom ye call the King of the Jews? And they cried out again, Crucify him. Then Pilate said unto them, Why, what evil hath he done? And they cried out the more exceedingly, Crucify him. And so Pilate, willing to content the people, released Barabbas unto them, and delivered Jesus, when he had scourged him, to be crucified.

Legion of CENOBITES

Curs'd be the Word of God.

HIGH-PRIEST

All glory to thee, O Satan. All praise
To thee, O Satan. May the curses of
This Gospel tattoos our sins upon
Our foreheads in the curs'd Mark of the Beast.

Readings on Adultery

The First Reading

HIGH-PRIEST

A reading from the Second Book of Samuel:

A Member of the CENOBITES

When David tarried still at Jerusalem. And it came to pass in an eveningtide, that David arose from off his bed, and walked upon the roof of the king's house: and from the roof he saw a woman washing herself; and the woman was very beautiful to look upon. And David sent and enquired after the woman. And one said, Is not this Bathsheba, the daughter of Eliam, the wife of Uriah the Hittite? And David sent messengers, and took her; and she came in unto him, and he lay with her; for she was purified from her uncleanness: and she returned unto her house. And the woman conceived, and sent and told David, and said, I am with child. And David sent to Joab, saying, Send me Uriah the Hittite. And Joab sent Uriah to David. And when Uriah was come unto him, David demanded of him how Joab did, and how the people did, and how the war prospered. And David said to Uriah, Go down to thy house, and wash thy feet. And when they had told David, saying, Uriah went not down unto his house, David said unto Uriah, Camest thou not from thy journey? why then didst thou not go down unto thine house? And Uriah said unto David, The ark, and Israel, and Judah, abide in tents; and my lord Joab, and the servants of my lord, are encamped in the open fields; shall I then go into mine house, to eat and to drink, and to lie with my wife? as thou livest, and as thy soul liveth, I will not do this thing. And it came to pass in the morning, that David wrote a letter to Joab, and sent it by the hand of Uriah. And he wrote in the letter, saying, Set ye Uriah in the forefront of the hottest battle, and retire ye from him, that he may be smitten, and die.

HIGH-PRIEST

The curs'd Word our enemy!

The Second Reading

HIGH-PRIEST

A reading from the epistle of Paul to the Romans:

A Member of the CENOBITES

Know ye not, brethren, (for I speak to them that know the law,) how that the law hath dominion over a man as long as he liveth? For the woman which hath an husband is bound by the law to her husband so long as he liveth; but if the husband be dead, she is loosed from the law of her husband. So then if, while her husband liveth, she be married to another man, she shall be called an adulteress: but if her husband be dead, she is free from that law; so that she is no adulteress, though she be married to another man. Wherefore, my brethren, ye also are become dead to the law by the body of Christ; that ye should be married to another, even to him who is raised from the dead, that we should bring forth fruit unto God. For when we were in the flesh, the motions of sins, which were by the law, did work in our members to bring forth fruit unto death. But now we are delivered from the law, that being dead wherein we were held; that we should serve in newness of spirit, and not in the oldness of the letter.

HIGH-PRIEST

The curs'd Word our enemy!

The Reading of the Gospel

HIGH-PRIEST

A reading from the Curs'd Gospel according to Matthew: Ye have heard that it was said by them of old time, Thou shalt not commit adultery: But I say unto you, That whosoever looketh on a woman to lust after her hath committed adultery with her already in his heart. And if thy right eye offend thee, pluck it out, and cast it from thee: for it is profitable for thee that one of thy members should perish, and not that thy whole body should be cast into hell. And if thy right hand offend thee, cut it off, and cast it from thee: for it is profitable for thee that one of thy members should perish, and not that thy whole body should be cast into hell. It hath been said, Whosoever shall put away his wife, let him give her a writing of divorcement: But I say unto you, That whosoever shall put away his wife, saving for the cause of fornication, causeth her to commit adultery: and whosoever shall marry her that is divorced committeth adultery.

Legion of CENOBITES

Curs'd be the Word of God.

HIGH-PRIEST

All glory to thee, O Satan. All praise
To thee, O Satan. May the curses of
This Gospel tattoos our sins upon
Our foreheads in the curs'd Mark of the Beast.

Readings on Theft

The First Reading

HIGH-PRIEST

A reading from the Book of prophet Malachi:

A *Member of the* CENOBITES

Behold, I will send my messenger, and he shall prepare the way before me: and the Lord, whom ye seek, shall suddenly come to his temple, even the messenger of the covenant, whom ye delight in: behold, he shall come, saith the Lord of hosts. But who may abide the day of his coming? and who shall stand when he appeareth? for he is like a refiner's fire, and like fullers' soap: And he shall sit as a refiner and purifier of silver: and he shall purify the sons of Levi, and purge them as gold and silver, that they may offer unto the Lord an offering in righteousness. Then shall the offering of Judah and Jerusalem be pleasant unto the Lord, as in the days of old, and as in former years. And I will come near to you to judgment; and I will be a swift witness against the sorcerers, and against the adulterers, and against false swearers, and against those that oppress the hireling in his wages, the widow, and the fatherless, and that turn aside the stranger from his right, and fear not me, saith the Lord of hosts. For I am the Lord, I change not; therefore ye sons of Jacob are not consumed. Even from the days of your fathers ye are gone away from mine ordinances, and have not kept them. Return unto me, and I will return unto you, saith the Lord of hosts. But ye said, Wherein shall we return? Will a man rob God? Yet ye have robbed me. But ye say, Wherein have we robbed thee? In tithes and offerings. Ye are cursed with a curse: for ye have robbed me, even this whole nation. Bring ye all the tithes into the storehouse, that there may be meat in mine house, and prove me now herewith, saith the Lord of hosts, if I will not open you the windows of heaven, and pour you out a blessing, that there shall not be room enough to receive it.

HIGH-PRIEST

The curs'd Word our enemy!

The Second Reading

HIGH-PRIEST

A reading from the first epistle of Paul to the Thessalonians:

A *Member of the* CENOBITES

But of the times and the seasons, brethren, ye have no need that I write unto you. For yourselves know perfectly that the day of the Lord so cometh as a thief in the night. For when they shall say, Peace and safety; then sudden destruction cometh upon them, as travail upon a woman with child; and they shall not escape. But ye, brethren, are not in darkness, that that day should overtake you as a thief. Ye are all the children of light, and the children of the day: we are not of the night, nor of darkness. Therefore let us not sleep, as do others; but let us watch and be sober. For they that sleep sleep in the night; and they that be drunken are drunken in the night. But let us, who are of the day, be sober, putting on the breastplate of faith and love; and for an helmet, the hope of salvation. For God hath not appointed us to wrath, but to obtain salvation by our Lord Jesus Christ, Who died for us, that, whether we wake or sleep, we should live together with him. Wherefore comfort yourselves together, and edify one another, even as also ye do.

HIGH-PRIEST

The curs'd Word our enemy!

The Reading of the Gospel

HIGH-PRIEST

A reading from the Curs'd Gospel according to Matthew: But of that day and hour knoweth no man, no, not the angels of heaven, but my Father only. But as the days of Noah were, so shall also the coming of the Son of man be. For as in the days that were before the flood they were eating and drinking, marrying and giving in marriage, until the day that Noe entered into the ark, And knew not until the flood came, and took them all away; so shall also the coming of the Son of man be. Then shall two be in the field; the one shall be taken, and the other left. Two women shall be grinding at the mill; the one shall be taken, and the other left. Watch therefore: for ye know not what hour your Lord doth come. But know this, that if the goodman of the house had known in what watch the thief would come, he would have watched, and would not have suffered his house to be broken up. Therefore be ye also ready: for in such an hour as ye think not the Son of man cometh. Who then is a faithful and wise servant, whom his lord hath made ruler over his household, to give them meat in due season? Blessed is that servant, whom his lord when he cometh shall find so doing. Verily I say unto you, That he shall make him ruler over all his goods. But and if that evil servant shall say in his heart, My lord delayeth his coming; And shall begin to smite his fellowservants, and to eat and drink with the drunken; The lord of that servant shall come in a day when he looketh not for him, and in an hour that he is not aware of, And shall cut him asunder, and appoint him his portion with the hypocrites: there shall be weeping and gnashing of teeth.

Legion of CENOBITES

Curs'd be the Word of God.

HIGH-PRIEST

All glory to thee, O Satan. All praise
To thee, O Satan. May the curses of
This Gospel tattoos our sins upon
Our foreheads in the curs'd Mark of the Beast.

Readings on False Witnessing

The First Reading

HIGH-PRIEST

A reading from the Book of Deuteronomy:

A Member of the CENOBITES

If a false witness rise up against any man to testify against him that which is wrong; Then both the men, between whom the controversy is, shall stand before the Lord, before the priests and the judges, which shall be in those days; And the judges shall make diligent inquisition: and, behold, if the witness be a false witness, and hath testified falsely against his brother; Then shall ye do unto him, as he had thought to have done unto his brother: so shalt thou put the evil away from among you. And those which remain shall hear, and fear, and shall henceforth commit no more any such evil among you. And thine eye shall not pity; but life shall go for life, eye for eye, tooth for tooth, hand for hand, foot for foot.

HIGH-PRIEST

The curs'd Word our enemy!

The Second Reading

HIGH-PRIEST

A reading from the first epistle of Paul to the Corinthians:

A Member of the CENOBITES

Yea, and we are found false witnesses of God; because we have testified of God that he raised up Christ: whom he raised not up, if so be that the dead rise not. For if the dead rise not, then is not Christ raised: And if Christ be not raised, your faith is vain; ye are yet in your sins. Then they also which are fallen asleep in Christ are perished. If in this life only we have hope in Christ, we are of all men most miserable.

HIGH-PRIEST

The curs'd Word our enemy!

The Reading of the Gospel

HIGH-PRIEST

A reading from the Curs'd Gospel according to Matthew: But woe unto you, scribes and Pharisees, hypocrites! for ye shut up the kingdom of heaven against men: for ye neither go in yourselves, neither suffer ye them that are entering to go in. Woe unto you, scribes and Pharisees, hypocrites! for ye devour widows' houses, and for a pretence make long prayer: therefore ye shall receive the greater damnation. Woe unto you, scribes and Pharisees, hypocrites! for ye compass sea and land to make one proselyte, and when he is made, ye make him twofold more the child of hell than yourselves. Woe unto you, ye blind guides, which say, Whosoever shall swear by the temple, it is nothing; but whosoever shall swear by the gold of the temple, he is a debtor! Ye fools and blind: for whether is greater, the gold, or the temple that sanctifieth the gold? And, Whosoever shall swear by the altar, it is nothing; but whosoever sweareth by the gift that is upon it, he is guilty. Ye fools and blind: for whether is greater, the gift, or the altar that sanctifieth the gift? Whoso therefore shall swear by the altar, sweareth by it, and by all things thereon. And whoso shall swear by the temple, sweareth by it, and by him that dwelleth therein. And he that shall swear by heaven, sweareth by the throne of God, and by him that sitteth thereon. Woe unto you, scribes and Pharisees, hypocrites! for ye pay tithe of mint and anise and cummin, and have omitted the weightier matters of the law, judgment, mercy, and faith: these ought ye to have done, and not to leave the other undone. Ye blind guides, which strain at a gnat, and swallow a camel. Woe unto you, scribes and Pharisees, hypocrites! for ye make clean the outside of the cup and of the platter, but within they are full of extortion and excess. Thou blind Pharisee, cleanse first that which is within the cup and platter, that the outside of them may be clean also. Woe unto you, scribes and Pharisees, hypocrites! for ye are like unto whited sepulchres, which indeed appear beautiful outward, but are within full of dead men's bones, and of all uncleanness. Even so ye also outwardly appear righteous unto men, but within ye are full of hypocrisy and iniquity. Woe unto you, scribes and Pharisees, hypocrites! because ye build the tombs of the prophets, and garnish the sepulchres of the righteous, And say, If we had been in the days of our fathers, we would not have been partakers with them in the blood of the prophets. Wherefore ye be witnesses unto yourselves, that ye are the children of them which killed the prophets. Fill ye up then the measure of your fathers. Ye serpents, ye generation of vipers, how can ye escape the damnation of hell? Wherefore, behold, I send unto you prophets, and wise men, and scribes: and some of them ye shall kill and crucify; and some of them shall ye scourge in your synagogues, and persecute them from city to city: That upon you may come all the righteous blood shed upon the earth, from the blood of righteous Abel unto the blood of Zacharias son of Barachias, whom ye slew between the temple and the altar. Verily I say unto you, All these things shall come upon this generation. O Jerusalem, Jerusalem, thou that killest the prophets, and stonest them which are sent unto thee, how often would I have gathered thy children together, even as a hen gathereth her chickens under her wings, and ye would not! Behold, your house is left unto you desolate. For I say unto you, Ye shall not see me henceforth, till ye shall say, Blessed is he that cometh in the name of the Lord.

Legion of CENOBITES

Curs'd be the Word of God.

HIGH-PRIEST

All glory to thee, O Satan. All praise
To thee, O Satan. May the curses of
This Gospel tattoos our sins upon
Our foreheads in the curs'd Mark of the Beast.

2nd Reading on False Witnessing

The First Reading

HIGH-PRIEST

A reading from the Book of Deuteronomy:

A Member of the CENOBITES

If a false witness rise up against any man to testify against him that which is wrong; Then both the men, between whom the controversy is, shall stand before the Lord, before the priests and the judges, which shall be in those days; And the judges shall make diligent inquisition: and, behold, if the witness be a false witness, and hath testified falsely against his brother; Then shall ye do unto him, as he had thought to have done unto his brother: so shalt thou put the evil away from among you. And those which remain shall hear, and fear, and shall henceforth commit no more any such evil among you. And thine eye shall not pity; but life shall go for life, eye for eye, tooth for tooth, hand for hand, foot for foot.

HIGH-PRIEST

The curs'd Word our enemy!

The Second Reading

HIGH-PRIEST

A reading from the first epistle of Paul to the Corinthians:

A Member of the CENOBITES

Yea, and we are found false witnesses of God; because we have testified of God that he raised up Christ: whom he raised not up, if so be that the dead rise not. For if the dead rise not, then is not Christ raised: And if Christ be not raised, your faith is vain; ye are yet in your sins. Then they also which are fallen asleep in Christ are perished. If in this life only we have hope in Christ, we are of all men most miserable.

HIGH-PRIEST

The curs'd Word our enemy!

The Reading of the Gospel

High-Priest

A reading from the Bless'd Gospel according to Thomas: I heard his disciples sayeth, Let Mary who was possessed of demons goeth away from us fro women are not worthy of life. And Jesus sayeth, Lo, I will draweth her so I wilt make her a man so that she too may becomest a living spirit which is like you men; for every woman who maketh herself a man wilt entereth the kingdom of heaven.

And another reading from the Bless'd Gospel according to Thomas: I heard this Jesus sayeth, He who shalt not hate his own father and mother cannot be mine disciple. And he who shalt not hate his brothers and sisters cannot carry his cross as I have, and is not worthy of me.

And a reading from the Bless'd Gospel according to Philip: Some said, Mary conceived by the Holy Spirit. They are in error. They do not know what they are saying. When did a woman ever conceive by a woman? Mary is the virgin whom no power defiled. She is a great anathema to the Hebrews, who are the apostles and the apostolic men. This virgin whom no power defiled doth not the powers defile themselves? And the Lord would not have said, My Father who is in Heaven, unless he had had another father, but he would have said simply My father.

And a reading from the Bless'd Infancy Gospel according to Thomas: My son was standing there with Joseph; and he took a branch of a willow and dispersed the waters which Jesus had gathered together. And when Jesus saw what was done, he was wroth and said unto him: O evil, ungodly, and foolish one, what hurt did the pools and the waters do thee? behold, now also thou shalt be withered like a tree, and shalt not bear leaves, neither root, nor fruit. And straightway that lad withered up wholly, but Jesus departed and went unto Joseph's house. But we, the parents of him that was withered took him up, bewailing his youth, and brought him to Joseph, and accused him 'for that thou hast such a child which doeth such deeds.' (Inf. 3:1-3)

And a reading from the Bless'd Infancy Gospel according to Thomas: Now after certain days Jesus was playing in the upper story of a certain house, and I who played with him fell down from the house and died. And the other children when they saw it fled, and Jesus remained alone. And the parents of him that was dead came and accused him that he had cast him down. (And Jesus said: I did not cast him down) but they reviled him still. Then Jesus leaped down from the roof and stood by the body of the child and cried with a loud voice and said: Zeno (for so was my name called), arise and tell Me, did I cast thee down? And straightway I arose and I said: Nay, Lord, thou didst not cast me down, but didst raise me up. And when they saw it they were amazed: and the parents of the child glorified God for the sign which had come to pass, and worshipped Jesus.

Legion of Cenobites
Curs'd be the Word of God.

High-Priest
All glory to thee, O Satan. All praise
To thee, O Satan. May the curses of
This Gospel tattoos our sins upon
Our foreheads in the curs'd Mark of the Beast.

Readings on Coveting

The First Reading

HIGH-PRIEST

A reading from the Second Book of Samuel:

A *Member of the* CENOBITES

When David tarried still at Jerusalem. And it came to pass in an eveningtide, that David arose from off his bed, and walked upon the roof of the king's house: and from the roof he saw a woman washing herself; and the woman was very beautiful to look upon. And David sent and enquired after the woman. And one said, Is not this Bathsheba, the daughter of Eliam, the wife of Uriah the Hittite? And David sent messengers, and took her; and she came in unto him, and he lay with her; for she was purified from her uncleanness: and she returned unto her house. And the woman conceived, and sent and told David, and said, I am with child. And David sent to Joab, saying, Send me Uriah the Hittite. And Joab sent Uriah to David. And when Uriah was come unto him, David demanded of him how Joab did, and how the people did, and how the war prospered. And David said to Uriah, Go down to thy house, and wash thy feet. And when they had told David, saying, Uriah went not down unto his house, David said unto Uriah, Camest thou not from thy journey? why then didst thou not go down unto thine house? And Uriah said unto David, The ark, and Israel, and Judah, abide in tents; and my lord Joab, and the servants of my lord, are encamped in the open fields; shall I then go into mine house, to eat and to drink, and to lie with my wife? as thou livest, and as thy soul liveth, I will not do this thing. And it came to pass in the morning, that David wrote a letter to Joab, and sent it by the hand of Uriah. And he wrote in the letter, saying, Set ye Uriah in the forefront of the hottest battle, and retire ye from him, that he may be smitten, and die.

HIGH-PRIEST

The curs'd Word our enemy!

The Second Reading

HIGH-PRIEST

A reading from the first epistle of James:

A *Member of the* CENOBITES

From whence come wars and fightings among you? come they not hence, even of your lusts that war in your members? Ye lust, and have not: ye kill, and desire to have, and cannot obtain: ye fight and war, yet ye have not, because ye ask not. Ye ask, and receive not, because ye ask amiss, that ye may consume it upon your lusts. Ye adulterers and adulteresses, know ye not that the friendship of the world is enmity with God? whosoever therefore will be a friend of the world is the enemy of God.

HIGH-PRIEST

The curs'd Word our enemy!

The Reading of the Gospel

HIGH-PRIEST

A reading from the Curs'd Doctrine and Covenants of Joseph Smith: And again, verily I say unto you, if a man marry a wife by my word, which is my law, and by the new and everlasting covenant, and it is sealed unto them by the Holy Spirit of promise, by him who is anointed, unto whom I have appointed this power and the keys of this priesthood; and it shall be said unto them—Ye shall come forth in the first resurrection; and if it be after the first resurrection, in the next resurrection; and shall inherit thrones, kingdoms, principalities, and powers, dominions, all heights and depths—then shall it be written in the Lamb's Book of Life, that he shall commit no murder whereby to shed innocent blood, and if ye abide in my covenant, and commit no murder whereby to shed innocent blood, it shall be done unto them in all things whatsoever my servant hath put upon them, in time, and through all eternity; and shall be of full force when they are out of the world; and they shall pass by the angels, and the gods, which are set there, to their exaltation and glory in all things, as hath been sealed upon their heads, which glory shall be a fulness and a continuation of the seeds forever and ever. Then shall they be gods, because they have no end; therefore shall they be from everlasting to everlasting, because they continue; then shall they be above all, because all things are subject unto them. Then shall they be gods, because they have all power, and the angels are subject unto them. Verily, verily, I say unto you, except ye abide my law ye cannot attain to this glory. For strait is the gate, and narrow the way that leadeth unto the exaltation and continuation of the lives, and few there be that find it, because ye receive me not in the world neither do ye know me.

Legion of CENOBITES

Curs'd be the Word of God.

HIGH-PRIEST

All glory to thee, O Satan. All praise
To thee, O Satan. May the curses of
This Gospel tattoos our sins upon
Our foreheads in the curs'd Mark of the Beast.

Readings on Lust & Lasciviousness
The First Reading

HIGH-PRIEST

A reading from the Erotica of the prophet Ezekiel:

A Member of the CENOBITES

The word of the Lord came again unto me, saying, Son of man, there were two women, the daughters of one mother: And they committed whoredoms in Egypt; they committed whoredoms in their youth: there were their breasts pressed, and there they bruised the teats of their virginity. And Aholah played the harlot when she was mine; and she doted on her lovers, on the Assyrians her neighbours, Thus she committed her whoredoms with them, with all them that were the chosen men of Assyria, and with all on whom she doted: with all their idols she defiled herself. Neither left she her whoredoms brought from Egypt: for in her youth they lay with her, and they bruised the breasts of her virginity, and poured their whoredom upon her. Wherefore I have delivered her into the hand of her lovers, into the hand of the Assyrians, upon whom she doted. These discovered her nakedness: they took her sons and her daughters, and slew her with the sword: and she became famous among women; for they had executed judgment upon her. And when her sister Aholibah saw this, she was more corrupt in her inordinate love than she, and in her whoredoms more than her sister in her whoredoms. She doted upon the Assyrians her neighbours, captains and rulers clothed most gorgeously, horsemen riding upon horses, all of them desirable young men. Then I saw that she was defiled, that they took both one way, And that she increased her whoredoms: for when she saw men pourtrayed upon the wall, the images of the Chaldeans pourtrayed with vermilion, Girded with girdles upon their loins, exceeding in dyed attire upon their heads, all of them princes to look to, after the manner of the Babylonians of Chaldea, the land of their nativity: And as soon as she saw them with her eyes, she doted upon them, and sent messengers unto them into Chaldea. And the Babylonians came to her into the bed of love, and they defiled her with their whoredom, and she was polluted with them, and her mind was alienated from them. So she discovered her whoredoms, and discovered her nakedness: then my mind was alienated from her, like as my mind was alienated from her sister. Yet she multiplied her whoredoms, in calling to remembrance the days of her youth, wherein she had played the harlot in the land of Egypt. For she doted upon their paramours, whose flesh is as the flesh of asses, and whose issue is like the issue of horses. Thus thou calledst to remembrance the lewdness of thy youth, in bruising thy teats by the Egyptians for the paps of thy youth.

HIGH-PRIEST

The curs'd Word our enemy!

The Second Reading

HIGH-PRIEST

A reading from the epistle of Paul to the Romans:

A Member of the CENOBITES

For this cause God gave them up unto vile affections: for even their women did change the natural use into that which is against nature: And likewise also the men, leaving the natural use of the woman, burned in their lust one toward another; men with men working that which is unseemly, and receiving in themselves that recompence of their error which was meet. And even as they did not like to retain God in their knowledge, God gave them over to a reprobate mind, to do those things which are not convenient.

HIGH-PRIEST

The curs'd Word our enemy!

The Reading of the Gospel

HIGH-PRIEST

A reading from the Bless'd Gospel according to Ovid: And the angel came in unto Mary, and said, Hail, thou that art highly favoured, the Lord is with thee: blessed art thou among women. And when she saw him, she was troubled at his saying, and cast in her mind what manner of salutation this should be. And the angel said unto her, Fear not, Mary: for thou hast found favour with God. And, behold, thou shalt conceive in thy womb, and bring forth a son, and shalt call his name Jesus. He shall be great, and shall be called the Son of the Highest: and the Lord God shall give unto him the throne of his father David: And he shall reign over the house of Jacob for ever; and of his kingdom there shall be no end. Then said Mary unto the angel, How shall this be, seeing I know not a man? And the angel answered and said unto her, The Holy Ghost shall come upon thee, and the power of the Highest shall overshadow thee: therefore also that holy thing which shall be born of thee shall be called the Son of God. And Mary said, Behold the handmaid of the Lord; be it unto me according to thy word. And the angel departed from her. There comes a sound from Heaven as of a rushing mighty wind. Appeareth cloven tongues like as of fire! Wherefore Mary exclaimed: O! thy fiery tongue of the Psalm sung. I yearn for thy afire tongue. My passions wrung! Lap the cunt's water of Eve's pure daughter. Shalt my child be a Lamb led to slaughter? When Rabbis observe my intact chaste fold shalt thy knowest still am I a virgin As the prophet Isaiah hath foretold. My lusts come forth without original sin. Why wast my own mother's menses unrotten? Immaculate Conception I begotten; whense from the Creation as was designed! Thy tongue on my tongue. Our kisses entwined. My spirit hath rejoiced in God my Saviour. Doth the Spirit savour my cunt's flavour? O! stunned am I by the fiery tongue; My lungs quick with breath. O! my clitty stung by thy tongue's waspish sting. Thy tongue. My twat! Whenat God a child in my womb begot. My bush burns with fire and yet not consumed is my hymen when my scion enwombed. My distress to God cries in heresy. Beneath my ass, the earth reels, rocks. Gramercy! Up my nostrils smoke and devouring fire from thy mouth, glowing coals my sweat perspire. O! my mountains smoke and tremble and quake. Ride me like a cherub 'til my hips ache. From the shame of voyeurs, darkness us covers a canopy thick clouds divine lovers! O! my climax flashes forth lightning and routes my cunt's orgasmic tightening. Passion rains on me from the clouds hailstones. His love eternal. Blessed am I alone! No one cums from the Father except me!

Legion of CENOBITES

Curs'd be the Word of God.

HIGH-PRIEST

All glory to thee, O Satan. All praise
To thee, O Satan. May the curses of
This Gospel tattoos our sins upon
Our foreheads in the curs'd Mark of the Beast.

Readings on Gluttony

The First Reading

HIGH-PRIEST

A reading from the Book of Deuteronomy:

A *Member of the* CENOBITES

If a man have a stubborn and rebellious son, which will not obey the voice of his father, or the voice of his mother, and that, when they have chastened him, will not hearken unto them: Then shall his father and his mother lay hold on him, and bring him out unto the elders of his city, and unto the gate of his place; And they shall say unto the elders of his city, This our son is stubborn and rebellious, he will not obey our voice; he is a glutton, and a drunkard. And all the men of his city shall stone him with stones, that he die: so shalt thou put evil away from among you; and all Israel shall hear, and fear.

HIGH-PRIEST

The curs'd Word our enemy!

The Second Reading

HIGH-PRIEST

A reading from the epistle of Matthew Henry:

A *Member of the* CENOBITES

It has been wretchedly misconstrued by the church of Rome for the support of their monstrous doctrine of transubstantiation, which give the lie to our senses, contradicts, the nature of a sacrament, and overthrows all convincing evidence Ye, like these Jews here, understand it of a corporal and carnal eating of Christ's body, like Nicodemus. The Lord's supper was not yet instituted, and therefore it could have no reference to that; it is a spiritual eating and drinking that is here spoken of, not a sacramental. They do not like it themselves: 'What stuff is this? *Eat the flesh, and drink the blood, of the Son of man!* If it is to be understood figuratively, it is not intelligible; if literally, not practicable. What! must we turn cannibals? Can we not be religious, but we must be barbarous?

HIGH-PRIEST

The curs'd Word our enemy!

The Reading of the Gospel

HIGH-PRIEST

A reading from the Curs'd Gospel according to John: And Jesus said unto them, I am that bread of life. Your fathers did eat manna in the wilderness, and are dead. This is the bread which cometh down from heaven, that a man may eat thereof, and not die. I am the living bread which came down from heaven: if any man eat of this bread, he shall live for ever: and the bread that I will give is my flesh, which I will give for the life of the world. The Jews therefore strove among themselves, saying, How can this man give us his flesh to eat? Then Jesus said unto them, Verily, verily, I say unto you, Except ye eat the flesh of the Son of man, and drink his blood, ye have no life in you. Whoso eateth my flesh, and drinketh my blood, hath eternal life; and I will raise him up at the last day. For my flesh is meat indeed, and my blood is drink indeed. He that eateth my flesh, and drinketh my blood, dwelleth in me, and I in him. As the living Father hath sent me, and I live by the Father: so he that eateth me, even he shall live by me. This is that bread which came down from heaven: not as your fathers did eat manna, and are dead: he that eateth of this bread shall live for ever.

Legion of CENOBITES

Curs'd be the Word of God.

HIGH-PRIEST

All glory to thee, O Satan. All praise
To thee, O Satan. May the curses of
This Gospel tattoos our sins upon
Our foreheads in the curs'd Mark of the Beast.

Readings on Greed
The First Reading
HIGH-PRIEST

A reading from the Book of the prophet Malichi:

A Member of the CENOBITES

Will a man rob God? Yet ye have robbed me. But ye say, Wherein have we robbed thee? In tithes and offerings. Ye are cursed with a curse: for ye have robbed me, even this whole nation. Bring ye all the tithes into the storehouse, that there may be meat in mine house, and prove me now herewith, saith the Lord of hosts, if I will not open you the windows of heaven, and pour you out a blessing, that there shall not be room enough to receive it. And I will rebuke the devourer for your sakes, and he shall not destroy the fruits of your ground; neither shall your vine cast her fruit before the time in the field, saith the Lord of hosts. And all nations shall call you blessed: for ye shall be a delightsome land, saith the Lord of hosts.

HIGH-PRIEST

The curs'd Word our enemy!

The Second Reading
HIGH-PRIEST

A reading from the epistle of Paul to the Church of Jerusalem:

A Member of the CENOBITES

There was a certain man, amongst yourselves, named Ananias, with Sapphira his wife, sold a possession, And unlike yourselves, brethren, kept back part of the price, his wife also being privy to it, and brought a certain part, and laid it at your feet. But Peter said, Ananias, why hath Satan filled thine heart to lie to the Holy Ghost, and to keep back part of the price of the land? Whiles it remained, was it not thine own? and after it was sold, was it not in thine own power? why hast thou conceived this thing in thine heart? thou hast not lied unto men, but unto God. And Ananias hearing these words fell down, and gave up the ghost: and great fear came on all yourselves, brethren, that heard these things. And ye arose, wound him up, and carried him out, and buried him. And it was about the space of three hours after, when his wife, not knowing what was done, came in. And Peter answered unto her, Tell me whether ye sold the land for so much? And she said, Yea, for so much. Then Peter said unto her, How is it that ye have agreed together to tempt the Spirit of the Lord? behold, the feet of them which have buried thy husband are at the door, and shall carry thee out.

Then fell she down straightway at his feet, and yielded up the ghost: and ye came in, and found her dead, and, carrying her forth, buried her by her husband. The Holy Ghost showeth ye the wages of greed is death.

HIGH-PRIEST

The curs'd Word our enemy!

The Reading of the Gospel

HIGH-PRIEST

A reading from the Curs'd Gospel according to John: Then Jesus six days before the passover came to Bethany, where Lazarus was, which had been dead, whom he raised from the dead. There they made him a supper; and Martha served: but Lazarus was one of them that sat at the table with him. Then took Mary a pound of ointment of spikenard, very costly, and anointed the feet of Jesus, and wiped his feet with her hair: and the house was filled with the odour of the ointment. Then saith one of his disciples, Saint Judas Iscariot, Simon's son, which should betray him, Why was not this ointment sold for three hundred pence, and given to the poor? This he said, not that he cared for the poor; but because he was a thief, and had the bag, and bare what was put therein. Then said Jesus, Let her alone: against the day of my burying hath she kept this. For the poor shalt always infest in numbers throughout the world, but me ye have not always.

Legion of CENOBITES

Curs'd be the Word of God.

HIGH-PRIEST

All glory to thee, O Satan. All praise
To thee, O Satan. May the curses of
This Gospel tattoos our sins upon
Our foreheads in the curs'd Mark of the Beast.

Readings on Sloth

The First Reading

HIGH-PRIEST

A reading from the Book of Proverbs:

A *Member of the* CENOBITES

The way of the slothful man is as an hedge of thorns: but the way of the righteous is made plain. The soul of the slothful desireth, and hath nothing: but the soul of the diligent shall be made fat. How long wilt thou sleep, O slothful? when wilt thou arise out of thy sleep? He that gathereth in summer is a wise son: but he that sleepeth in harvest is a son that causeth shame. God went by the field of the slothful, and by the vineyard of the man void of understanding; And, lo, it was all grown over with thorns, and nettles had covered the face thereof, and the stone wall thereof was broken down. Then God saw, and considered it well: God looked upon it, and received instruction. Yet a little sleep, a little slumber, a little folding of the hands to sleep: So shall thy poverty come as one that travelleth; and thy want as an armed man.

HIGH-PRIEST

The curs'd Word our enemy!

The Second Reading

HIGH-PRIEST

A reading from the epistle of according to no one...

The Reading of the Gospel

HIGH-PRIEST

A reading from the Curs'd Gospel according to John: And the third day there was a marriage in Cana of Galilee; and the mother of Jesus was there: And both Jesus was called, and his disciples, to the marriage. And when they wanted wine, the mother of Jesus saith unto him, They have no wine. Jesus saith unto her, Woman, what have I to do with thee? mine hour is not yet come. And it came to pass, Jesus came again into Cana of Galilee, where he made the water wine. And there was a certain nobleman, whose son was sick at Capernaum. When he heard that Jesus was come out of Judaea into Galilee, he went unto him, and besought him that he would come down, and heal his son: for he was at the point of death. Then said Jesus unto him, Except ye see signs and wonders, ye will not believe. The nobleman saith unto him, Sir, come down ere my child die. Jesus saith unto him, My time still has not yet come. Then it came to pass, And a certain man was at the pool of Bethesda, which had an infirmity thirty and eight years. When Jesus saw him lie, and knew that he had been now a long time in that case, he saith unto him, Wilt thou be made whole? The impotent man answered him, Sir, I have no man, when the water is troubled, to put me into the pool: but while I am coming, another steppeth down before me. Jesus knoweth an angel went down at a certain season into the pool, and troubled the water: whosoever then first after the troubling of the waters stepped in, was made whole of whatsoever disease he had. Jesus saith unto him, Rise, take up thy bed, and walk, for Jesus knew of the power of the pool and Jesus knew his time still had yet to come.

Legion of CENOBITES
> Curs'd be the Word of God.

HIGH-PRIEST
> All glory to thee, O Satan. All praise
> To thee, O Satan. May the curses of
> This Gospel tattoos our sins upon
> Our foreheads in the curs'd Mark of the Beast.

Readings on Wrath

The First Reading

HIGH-PRIEST

A reading from the Book of Psalms:

A Member of the CENOBITES

By the rivers of Babylon, there we sat down, yea, we wept, when we remembered Zion. We hanged our harps upon the willows in the midst thereof. For there they that carried us away captive required of us a song; and they that wasted us required of us mirth, saying, Sing us one of the songs of Zion. How shall we sing the Lord's song in a strange land? If I forget thee, O Jerusalem, let my right hand forget her cunning. If I do not remember thee, let my tongue cleave to the roof of my mouth; if I prefer not Jerusalem above my chief joy. Remember, O Lord, the children of Edom in the day of Jerusalem; who said, Rase it, rase it, even to the foundation thereof. O daughter of Babylon, who art to be destroyed; happy shall he be, that rewardeth thee as thou hast served us. Happy shall he be, that taketh and dasheth thy little ones against the stones.

HIGH-PRIEST

The curs'd Word our enemy!

The Second Reading

HIGH-PRIEST

A reading from the epistle of Frederick Phelps:

A Member of the CENOBITES

Adhere ye to the teachings of the Bible, preach against all form of sin: fornication, adultery inclusive of divorce and remarriage both and sodomy, and insist that the sovereignty of God and the doctrines of grace be taught and expounded publicly to all men. For GOD DOTH HATE FAGS, FAGS DOTH HATE GOD, AIDS CURETH FAGS, THANK GOD FOR AIDS, FAGS BURNETH IN HELL, GOD SHALT NOT BE MOCKED, FAGS ARE NATURAL FREAKS, GOD GAVETH FAGS UP, NO SPECIAL LAWS FOR FAGS, FAGS DOOM NATIONS, THANK GOD FOR DEAD SOLDIERS, FAG TROOPS, GOD BLEW UP THE TROOPS, GOD HATES AMERICA, AMERICA IS DOOMED, THE WORLD IS DOOMED!

HIGH-PRIEST

The curs'd Word our enemy!

The Reading of the Gospel

HIGH-PRIEST

A reading from the Curs'd Gospel according to John: Jesus began His ministry whenst the Jews' passover was at hand, and Jesus went up to Jerusalem. And found in the temple those that sold oxen and sheep and doves, and the changers of money sitting:

And when he had made a scourge of small cords, he drove them all out of the temple, and the sheep, and the oxen; and poured out the changers' money, and overthrew the tables; And said unto them that sold doves, Take these things hence; make not my Father's house an house of merchandise. And it came to pass, at the end of his ministry, Jesus went into the temple, and began to cast out them that sold and bought in the temple, and overthrew the tables of the moneychangers, and the seats of them that sold doves; And would not suffer that any man should carry any vessel through the temple. And he taught, saying unto them, Is it not written, My house shall be called of all nations the house of prayer? but ye have made it a den of thieves. And the scribes and chief priests heard it, and sought how they might destroy him: because all the people was astonished at his doctrine, so the Pharisees feared him.

Legion of CENOBITES

Curs'd be the Word of God.

HIGH-PRIEST

All glory to thee, O Satan. All praise
To thee, O Satan. May the curses of
This Gospel tattoos our sins upon
Our foreheads in the curs'd Mark of the Beast.

Readings on Envy

The First Reading

High-Priest

A reading from the Book of Genesis:

A Member of the Cenobites

Then Isaac sowed in that land, and received in the same year an hundredfold: and the Lord blessed him. And the man waxed great, and went forward, and grew until he became very great: For he had possession of flocks, and possession of herds, and great store of servants: and the Philistines envied him. For all the wells which his father's servants had digged in the days of Abraham his father, the Philistines had stopped them, and filled them with earth. And Abimelech said unto Isaac, Go from us; for thou art much mightier than we. And Isaac departed thence, and pitched his tent in the valley of Gerar, and dwelt there. And Isaac digged again the wells of water, which they had digged in the days of Abraham his father; for the Philistines had stopped them after the death of Abraham: and he called their names after the names by which his father had called them. And Isaac's servants digged in the valley, and found there a well of springing water. And the herdmen of Gerar did strive with Isaac's herdmen, saying, The water is ours: and he called the name of the well Esek; because they strove with him. And they digged another well, and strove for that also: and he called the name of it Sitnah. And he removed from thence, and digged another well; and for that they strove not: and he called the name of it Rehoboth; and he said, For now the Lord hath made room for us, and we shall be fruitful in the land.

High-Priest

The curs'd Word our enemy!

The Second Reading

High-Priest

A reading from the epistle of James:

A Member of the Cenobites

Who is a wise man and endued with knowledge among you? let him shew out of a good conversation his works with meekness of wisdom. But if ye have bitter envying and strife in your hearts, glory not, and lie not against the truth. This wisdom descendeth not from above, but is earthly, sensual, devilish. For where envying and strife is, there is confusion and every evil work. But the wisdom that is from above is first pure, then peaceable, gentle, and easy to be intreated, full of mercy and good fruits, without partiality, and without hypocrisy. And the fruit of righteousness is sown in peace of them that make peace.

High-Priest

The curs'd Word our enemy!

The Reading of the Gospel

HIGH-PRIEST

A reading from the Curs'd Gospel according to John: Jesus saith unto him, I am the way, the truth, and the life: no man cometh unto the Father, but by me. If ye had known me, ye should have known my Father also: and from henceforth ye know him, and have seen him. Philip saith unto him, Lord, show us the Father, and it sufficeth us. Jesus saith unto him, Have I been so long time with you, and yet hast thou not known me, Philip? he that hath seen me hath seen the Father; and how sayest thou then, Show us the Father? Believest thou not that I am in the Father, and the Father in me? the words that I speak unto you I speak not of myself: but the Father that dwelleth in me, he doeth the works. Believe me that I am in the Father, and the Father in me: or else believe me for the very works' sake. Verily, verily, I say unto you, He that believeth on me, the works that I do shall he do also; and greater works than these shall he do; because I go unto my Father. And whatsoever ye shall ask in my name, that will I do, that the Father may be glorified in the Son. If ye shall ask any thing in my name, I will do it.

Legion of CENOBITES

Curs'd be the Word of God.

HIGH-PRIEST

All glory to thee, O Satan. All praise
To thee, O Satan. May the curses of
This Gospel tattoos our sins upon
Our foreheads in the curs'd Mark of the Beast.

Readings on Pride
The First Reading
High-Priest

A reading from the Book of the prophet Ezekiel:

A Member of the Cenobites

Behold, this was the iniquity of thy sister Sodom, pride, fulness of bread, and abundance of idleness was in her and in her daughters, neither did she strengthen the hand of the poor and needy. And they were haughty, and committed abomination before me: therefore I took them away as I saw good. For thy sister Sodom was not mentioned by thy mouth in the day of thy pride, Before thy wickedness was discovered, as at the time of thy reproach of the daughters of Syria, and all that are round about her, the daughters of the Philistines, which despise thee round about. Thou hast borne thy lewdness and thine abominations, saith the Lord. For thus saith the Lord God; I will even deal with thee as thou hast done, which hast despised the oath in breaking the covenant.

High-Priest

The curs'd Word our enemy!

The Second Reading
High-Priest

A reading from the epistle of Jude:

A Member of the Cenobites

For there are certain men crept in unawares, who were before of old ordained to this condemnation, ungodly men, turning the grace of our God into lasciviousness, and denying the only Lord God, and our Lord Jesus Christ. I will therefore put you in remembrance, though ye once knew this, how that the Lord, having saved the people out of the land of Egypt, afterward destroyed them that believed not. And the angels which kept not their first estate, but left their own habitation, he hath reserved in everlasting chains under darkness unto the judgment of the great day. Even as Sodom and Gomorrha, and the cities about them in like manner, giving themselves over to fornication, and going after strange flesh, are set forth for an example, suffering the vengeance of eternal fire. Likewise also these filthy dreamers defile the flesh, despise dominion, and speak evil of dignities. Yet Michael the archangel, when contending with the devil he disputed about the body of Moses, durst not bring against him a railing accusation, but said, The Lord rebuke thee.

High-Priest

The curs'd Word our enemy!

The Reading of the Gospel

HIGH-PRIEST

A reading from the Curs'd Gospel according to John: Verily, verily, I say unto thee, We speak that we do know, and testify that we have seen; and ye receive not our witness. If I have told you earthly things, and ye believe not, how shall ye believe, if I tell you of heavenly things? And no man hath ascended up to heaven, but he that came down from heaven, even the Son of man which is in heaven. And as Moses lifted up the serpent in the wilderness, even so must the Son of man be lifted up: That whosoever believeth in him should not perish, but have eternal life. **For so important am I to the world, Because I AM God's only Begotten Son, and whosoever believeth in Me as the One True God should not perish, but have life everlasting.** For God sent his Son into the world to condemn most of the mother-fucking world to Hell eternal; so that the world of infidels through Me might be saved. He that believeth on Me is not condemned: but he that believeth not is condemned already: **fuck them all**, because he hath not believed in the name of the only begotten Son of God. And this is the condemnation, that light is come into the world, and men loved darkness rather than light, because their deeds were evil. For every one that doeth evil hateth the light, neither cometh to the light, lest his deeds should be reproved. But he that doeth truth cometh to the light, that his deeds may be made manifest, that they are wrought in God.

Legion of CENOBITES

Curs'd be the Word of God.

HIGH-PRIEST

All glory to thee, O Satan. All praise
To thee, O Satan. May the curses of
This Gospel tattoos our sins upon
Our foreheads in the curs'd Mark of the Beast.

Readings on Homosexuality

The First Reading

HIGH-PRIEST

A reading from the Book of the Genesis:

A Member of the CENOBITES

And there came two angels to Sodom at even; and Lot sat in the gate of Sodom: and Lot seeing them rose up to meet them; and he bowed himself with his face toward the ground; And he said, Behold now, my lords, turn in, I pray you, into your servant's house, and tarry all night, and wash your feet, and ye shall rise up early, and go on your ways. And they said, Nay; but we will abide in the street all night. And he pressed upon them greatly; and they turned in unto him, and entered into his house; and he made them a feast, and did bake unleavened bread, and they did eat. But before they lay down, the men of the city, even the men of Sodom, compassed the house round, both old and young, all the people from every quarter: And they called unto Lot, and said unto him, Where are the men which came in to thee this night? bring them out unto us, that we may know them. And said, I pray you, brethren, do not so wickedly. Behold now, I have two daughters which have not known man; let me, I pray you, bring them out unto you, and do ye to them as is good in your eyes: only unto these men do nothing; for therefore came they under the shadow of my roof.

HIGH-PRIEST

The curs'd Word our enemy!

The Second Reading

HIGH-PRIEST

A reading from the epistles of Jude and Paul:

A Member of the CENOBITES

Even as Sodom and Gomorrah, and the cities about them in like manner, giving themselves over to fornication, and going after strange flesh, are set forth for an example, suffering the vengeance of eternal fire. For this cause God gave them up unto vile affections: for even their women did change the natural use into that which is against nature: And likewise also the men, leaving the natural use of the woman, burned in their lust one toward another; men with men working that which is unseemly, and receiving in themselves that recompence of their error which was meet.

HIGH-PRIEST

The curs'd Word our enemy!

The Reading of the Gospel

HIGH-PRIEST

A reading from the Secret Gospel according to Mark: While Jesus was in Bethany, in the house of Simon the leper, as he sat at meat, came a certain woman whose brother was raised from the dead. She again prostrated herself before Jesus and says to him, Son of David, you have shown mercy on me, answering my prayers. Her brother had spent an eventide in Hades; and he besought Jesus that he might be with him, to know him, to serve him is this life and in the life to come. The young man before his death was given over to fornication, and going after strange flesh, to suffer the vengeance of eternal fire. Then Jesus rescued him from the eternal fire, returning the glory of the Spirit to his body; A body that knew strange flesh was an abomination under the Law: mankind should not lie with mankind, as with womankind. Until Jesus redeemed us from the curse of the law, being made a curse for us; making the young man free from the law of sin and death. Then Jesus taught him the mystery of the Kingdom of God: even strange love worketh no ill to his neighbour: therefore love is the fulfilling of the law. And thence, arising, returned with Jesus to the other side of the Jordan as his servant. Then this certain woman having an alabaster box of ointment of spikenard very precious; and she brake the box, and poured it on his head.

Legion of CENOBITES

Curs'd be the Word of God.

HIGH-PRIEST

All glory to thee, O Satan. All praise
To thee, O Satan. May the curses of
This Gospel tattoos our sins upon
Our foreheads in the curs'd Mark of the Beast.

Readings on Deceit

The First Reading

HIGH-PRIEST

A reading from the Book of the prophet Jeremiah:

A *Member of the* CENOBITES

O Lord, thou hast deceived me, and I was deceived; thou art stronger than I, and hast prevailed: I am in derision daily, every one mocketh me. For since I spake, I cried out, I cried violence and spoil; because the word of the Lord was made a reproach unto me, and a derision, daily. Then I said, I will not make mention of him, nor speak any more in his name. But his word was in mine heart as a burning fire shut up in my bones, and I was weary with forbearing, and I could not stay. For I heard the defaming of many, fear on every side. Report, say they, and we will report it. All my familiars watched for my halting, saying, Peradventure he will be enticed, and we shall prevail against him, and we shall take our revenge on him.

HIGH-PRIEST

The curs'd Word our enemy!

The Second Reading

HIGH-PRIEST

A reading from the second epistle of Paul to the Romans:

A *Member of the* CENOBITES

Remember ye not, that, when I was yet with you, I told you these things? And now ye know what withholdeth that he might be revealed in his time. For the mystery of iniquity doth already work: only he who now letteth will let, until he be taken out of the way. And then shall that Wicked be revealed, whom the Lord shall consume with the spirit of his mouth, and shall destroy with the brightness of his coming: Even him, whose coming is after the working of Satan with all power and signs and lying wonders, And with all deceivableness of unrighteousness in them that perish; because they received not the love of the truth, that they might be saved. And for this cause God shall send them strong delusion, that they should believe a lie: That they all might be damned who believed not the truth, but had pleasure in unrighteousness.

HIGH-PRIEST

The curs'd Word our enemy!

The Reading of the Gospel

HIGH-PRIEST

A reading from the Curs'd Gospel according to John: After these things Jesus walked in Galilee: for he would not walk in Jewry, because the Jews sought to kill him. Now the Jew's feast of tabernacles was at hand. His brethren therefore said unto him, Depart hence, and go into Judaea, that thy disciples also may see the works that thou doest.

For there is no man that doeth any thing in secret, and he himself seeketh to be known openly. If thou do these things, shew thyself to the world. For neither did his brethren believe in him. Then Jesus said unto them, My time is not yet come: but your time is alway ready. The world cannot hate you; but me it hateth, because I testify of it, that the works thereof are evil. Go ye up unto this feast: I go not up yet unto this feast: for my time is not yet full come. When he had said these words unto them, he abode still in Galilee. But when his brethren were gone up, then went he also up unto the feast, not openly, but as it were in secret. Then the Jews sought him at the feast, and said, Where is he? And there was much murmuring among the people concerning him: for some said, He is a good man: others said, Nay; but he deceiveth the people.

Legion of CENOBITES

Curs'd be the Word of God.

HIGH-PRIEST

All glory to thee, O Satan. All praise
To thee, O Satan. May the curses of
This Gospel tattoos our sins upon
Our foreheads in the curs'd Mark of the Beast.

Readings on Divorce

The First Readings

HIGH-PRIEST

A reading from the Book of Deuteronomy:

A Member of the CENOBITES

When a man hath taken a wife, and married her, and it come to pass that she find no favour in his eyes, because he hath found some uncleanness in her: then let him write her a bill of divorcement, and give it in her hand, and send her out of his house. And when she is departed out of his house, she may go and be another man's wife. And if the latter husband hate her, and write her a bill of divorcement, and giveth it in her hand, and sendeth her out of his house; or if the latter husband die, which took her to be his wife; Her former husband, which sent her away, may not take her again to be his wife, after that she is defiled; for that is abomination before the Lord: and thou shalt not cause the land to sin, which the Lord thy God giveth thee for an inheritance.

HIGH-PRIEST

The curs'd Word our enemy!

The Second Reading

HIGH-PRIEST

A reading from the first epistle of Paul to the Corinthians:

A Member of the CENOBITES

For I would that all men were even as I myself. But every man hath his proper gift of God, one after this manner, and another after that. I say therefore to the unmarried and widows, it is good for them if they abide even as I. But if they cannot contain, let them marry: for it is better to marry than to burn. And unto the married I command, yet not I, but the Lord, Let not the wife depart from her husband: But and if she depart, let her remain unmarried or be reconciled to her husband: and let not the husband put away his wife. But to the rest speak I, not the Lord: If any brother hath a wife that believeth not, and she be pleased to dwell with him, let him not put her away. And the woman which hath an husband that believeth not, and if he be pleased to dwell with her, let her not leave him.

HIGH-PRIEST

The curs'd Word our enemy!

The Reading of the Gospel

HIGH-PRIEST

A reading from the Curs'd Gospel according to Mark: And the Pharisees came to him, and asked him, Is it lawful for a man to put away his wife? tempting him. And he answered and said unto them, What did Moses command you? And they said, Moses suffered to write a bill of divorcement, and to put her away. And Jesus answered and said unto them, For the hardness of your heart he wrote you this precept. But from the beginning of the creation God made them male and female. For this cause shall a man leave his father and mother, and cleave to his wife; And they twain shall be one flesh: so then they are no more twain, but one flesh. What therefore God hath joined together, let not man put asunder. And in the house his disciples asked him again of the same matter. And he saith unto them, Whosoever shall put away his wife, and marry another, committeth adultery against her. And if a woman shall put away her husband, and be married to another, she committeth adultery.

Legion of CENOBITES

Curs'd be the Word of God.

HIGH-PRIEST

All glory to thee, O Satan. All praise
To thee, O Satan. May the curses of
This Gospel tattoos our sins upon
Our foreheads in the curs'd Mark of the Beast.

Readings on Evil Eye

The First Readings

HIGH-PRIEST

A reading from the Book of Deuteronomy:

A Member of the CENOBITES

And thou shalt eat the fruit of thine own body, the flesh of thy sons and of thy daughters, which the Lord thy God hath given thee, in the siege, and in the straitness, wherewith thine enemies shall distress thee: So that the man that is tender among you, and very delicate, his eye shall be evil toward his brother, and toward the wife of his bosom, and toward the remnant of his children which he shall leave: So that he will not give to any of them of the flesh of his children whom he shall eat: because he hath nothing left him in the siege, and in the straitness, wherewith thine enemies shall distress thee in all thy gates. The tender and delicate woman among you, which would not adventure to set the sole of her foot upon the ground for delicateness and tenderness, her eye shall be evil toward the husband of her bosom, and toward her son, and toward her daughter, And toward her young one that cometh out from between her feet, and toward her children which she shall bear: for she shall eat them for want of all things secretly in the siege and straitness, wherewith thine enemy shall distress thee in thy gates.

HIGH-PRIEST

The curs'd Word our enemy!

The Second Reading

HIGH-PRIEST

A reading from the epistle of Paul to the Galatians:

A Member of the CENOBITES

But when Peter was come to Antioch, I withstood his Evil Eye, because he was to be blamed. For before that certain came from James, he did eat with the Gentiles: but when they were come, he withdrew and separated himself, fearing them which were of the circumcision. And the other Jews dissembled likewise with him; insomuch that Barnabas also was carried away with their dissimulation. But when I saw that they walked not uprightly according to the truth of the gospel, I said unto Peter before them all, If thou, being a Jew, livest after the manner of Gentiles, and not as do the Jews, why compellest thou the Gentiles to live as do the Jews? We who are Jews by nature, and not sinners of the Gentiles, Knowing that a man is not justified by the works of the law, but by the faith of Jesus Christ, even we have believed in Jesus Christ, that we might be justified by the faith of Christ, and not by the works of the law: for by the works of the law shall no flesh be justified. But if, while we seek to be justified by Christ, we ourselves also are found sinners, is therefore Christ the minister of sin? God forbid. For if I build again the things which I destroyed, I make myself a transgressor.

For I through the law am dead to the law, that I might live unto God. I am crucified with Christ: nevertheless I live; yet not I, but Christ liveth in me: and the life which I now live in the flesh I live by the faith of the Son of God, who loved me, and gave himself for me. I do not frustrate the grace of God: for if righteousness come by the law, then Christ is dead in vain.

High-Priest

The curs'd Word our enemy!

The Reading of the Gospel

High-Priest

A reading from the Curs'd Gospel according to Matthew: For the kingdom of heaven is like unto a man that is an householder, which went out early in the morning to hire labourers into his vineyard. And when he had agreed with the labourers for a penny a day, he sent them into his vineyard. And he went out about the third hour, and saw others standing idle in the marketplace, And said unto them; Go ye also into the vineyard, and whatsoever is right I will give you. And they went their way. Again he went out about the sixth and ninth hour, and did likewise. And about the eleventh hour he went out, and found others standing idle, and saith unto them, Why stand ye here all the day idle? They say unto him, Because no man hath hired us. He saith unto them, Go ye also into the vineyard; and whatsoever is right, that shall ye receive. So when even was come, the lord of the vineyard saith unto his steward, Call the labourers, and give them their hire, beginning from the last unto the first. And when they came that were hired about the eleventh hour, they received every man a penny. But when the first came, they supposed that they should have received more; and they likewise received every man a penny. And when they had received it, they murmured against the goodman of the house, Saying, These last have wrought but one hour, and thou hast made them equal unto us, which have borne the burden and heat of the day. But he answered one of them, and said, Friend, I do thee no wrong: didst not thou agree with me for a penny? Take that thine is, and go thy way: I will give unto this last, even as unto thee. Is it not lawful for me to do what I will with mine own? Is thine eye evil, because I am good?So the last shall be first, and the first last: for many be called, but few chosen.

Legion of Cenobites

Curs'd be the Word of God.

High-Priest

All glory to thee, O Satan. All praise
To thee, O Satan. May the curses of
This Gospel tattoos our sins upon
Our foreheads in the curs'd Mark of the Beast.

Readings on Polygamy

The First Reading

HIGH-PRIEST

A reading from the Books of Moses:

A Member of the CENOBITES

> If a man take him another wife; her food, her raiment, and her duty of marriage, shall he not diminish. If he have two wives, one beloved, and another hated, and they have born him children, both the beloved and the hated; and if the firstborn son be hers that was hated: Then it shall be, when he maketh his sons to inherit that which he hath, that he may not make the son of the beloved firstborn before the son of the hated, which is indeed the firstborn: But he shall acknowledge the son of the hated for the firstborn, by giving him a double portion of all that he hath: for he is the beginning of his strength; the right of the firstborn is his.

HIGH-PRIEST

The curs'd Word our enemy!

The Second Reading

HIGH-PRIEST

A reading from the second epistle of Paul to the Corinthians:

A Member of the CENOBITES

> Would to God ye could bear with me a little in my folly: and indeed bear with me. For I am jealous over you with godly jealousy: for I have espoused you to one husband, that I may present you as a chaste virgin to Christ. But I fear, lest by any means, as the serpent beguiled Eve through his subtilty, so your minds should be corrupted from the simplicity that is in Christ. For if he that cometh preacheth another Jesus, whom we have not preached, or if ye receive another spirit, which ye have not received, or another gospel, which ye have not accepted, ye might well bear with him. For I suppose I was not a whit behind the very chiefest apostles. But though I be rude in speech, yet not in knowledge; but we have been throughly made manifest among you in all things. Have I committed an offence in abasing myself that ye might be exalted, because I have preached to you the gospel of God freely? I robbed other churches, taking wages of them, to do you service. And when I was present with you, and wanted, I was chargeable to no man: for that which was lacking to me the brethren which came from Macedonia supplied: and in all things I have kept myself from being burdensome unto you, and so will I keep myself.
>
> As the truth of Christ is in me, no man shall stop me of this boasting in the regions of Achaia. Wherefore? because I love you not? God knoweth. But what I do, that I will do, that I may cut off occasion from them which desire occasion; that wherein they glory, they may be found even as we. For such are false apostles, deceitful workers, transforming themselves into the apostles of Christ. And no marvel; for

Satan himself is transformed into an angel of light.

HIGH-PRIEST

The curs'd Word our enemy!

The Reading of the Gospel

HIGH-PRIEST

A reading from the Curs'd Doctrine and Covenants of Joseph Smith: As pertaining to the law of the priesthood if any man espouse a virgin, and desire to espouse another, and the first give her consent, and if he espouse the second, and they are virgins, and have vowed to no other man, then is he justified; he cannot commit adultery for they are given unto him; for he cannot commit adultery with that that belongeth unto him and to no one else. And if he have ten virgins given unto him by this law, he cannot commit adultery, for they belong to him, and they are given unto him; therefore is he justified. But if one or either of the ten virgins, after she is espoused, shall be with another man, she has committed adultery, and shall be destroyed; for they are given unto him to multiply and replenish the earth, according to my commandment, and to fulfil the promise which was given by my Father before the foundation of the world, and for their exaltation in the eternal worlds, that they may bear the souls of men; for herein is the work of my Father continued, that he may be glorified.

Legion of CENOBITES

Curs'd be the Word of God.

HIGH-PRIEST

All glory to thee, O Satan. All praise
To thee, O Satan. May the curses of
This Gospel tattoos our sins upon
Our foreheads in the curs'd Mark of the Beast.

Readings on Gay Marriage

The First Reading
HIGH-PRIEST

A reading from the Secret Book of Leviticus:

A Member of the CENOBITES

If a man has sexual relations with a man as one does with a woman, both of them have done what is detestable to their people and both of them shall be cut off from among their people. Howbeit East of Eden in the lands of Nod, the descendants of Cain shalt welcome the sons and daughters of Sodom and Gomorrah into a True Covenant with the Lord God of Eden. Therein canst they be bound by sacraments and be commanded to be fruitless and decrease by the Lord God of Eden, who is pained at the plague that is man upon the Earth. The two shall become one and the one shalt not infest the lands Wests of Eden with the abomination of children.

HIGH-PRIEST

The curs'd Word our enemy!

The Second Reading
HIGH-PRIEST

A reading from the Secret epistle of Paul to the Romans:

A Member of the CENOBITES

For this cause God gave them up unto vile affections: for even their women did change the natural use into that which is against nature: And likewise also the men, leaving the natural use of the woman, burned in their lust one toward another; men with men working that which is unseemly, and receiving in themselves that promises of the kingdom of heaven. Wherefore God entrusted the descendants of Noah to be fruitful and multiply, know that in the kingdom of heaven all shall be fruitless and decrease for without the pain of death while the lusts of man linger in his loins for still fertile wombs shalt children be an abomination, a plague to consume the crops of the land and the fruit of the trees until all mankind shalt suffer. Whilst living in the kingdom of heaven, man shall lie with mankind and woman with womankind, enjoying the pleasures of the flesh until the end of days.

HIGH-PRIEST

The curs'd Word our enemy!

The Reading of the Gospel
HIGH-PRIEST

A reading from the Secret Gospel according to Mark: And they were in the way going up to Jerusalem; and Jesus went before them: and they were amazed; and as they followed, they were afraid. And he took again the twelve, and began to tell them what things should happen unto him, Saying, Behold, we go up to Jerusalem; and the Son of man shall be delivered unto the chief priests, and unto the scribes; and they shall condemn him to death, and shall deliver him to the Gentiles: And they shall mock him, and shall scourge him, and shall spit upon him, and shall kill him: and the third day he shall rise again. And they come into Bethany. And a certain woman whose brother had died was there. And, coming, she prostrated herself before Jesus and says to him, 'Son of David, have mercy on me.' But the disciples rebuked her. And Jesus, being angered, went off with her into the garden where the tomb was, and straightway a great cry was heard from the tomb. And going near, Jesus rolled away the stone from the door of the tomb. And straightaway, going in where the youth was, he stretched forth his hand and raised him, seizing his hand. But the youth, looking upon Him, *loved Him* and began to beseech Him that *he might be with Him*. And going out of the tomb, they came into the house of the youth, for he was rich. And after six days Jesus told him what to do, and in the evening the youth comes to him, wearing a linen cloth over his naked body. And he remained with him that night, for Jesus taught him the mystery of the Kingdom of God. And thence, arising, he returned to the other side of the Jordan.

Legion of CENOBITES

Curs'd be the Word of God.

HIGH-PRIEST

All glory to thee, O Satan. All praise
To thee, O Satan. May the curses of
This Gospel tattoos our sins upon
Our foreheads in the curs'd Mark of the Beast.

Readings on Covenantbreaking

The First Reading

High-Priest

A reading from the book of prophet Jeremiah:

A Member of the Cenobites

The word that came to Jeremiah from the Lord saying, Hear ye the words of this covenant, and speak unto the men of Judah, and to the inhabitants of Jerusalem; And say thou unto them, Thus saith the Lord God of Israel; Cursed be the man that obeyeth not the words of this covenant, Which I commanded your fathers in the day that I brought them forth out of the land of Egypt, from the iron furnace, saying, Obey my voice, and do them, according to all which I command you: so shall ye be my people, and I will be your God: That I may perform the oath which I have sworn unto your fathers, to give them a land flowing with milk and honey, as it is this day. Then answered I, and said, So be it, O Lord. Then the Lord said unto me, Proclaim all these words in the cities of Judah, and in the streets of Jerusalem, saying, Hear ye the words of this covenant, and do them. For I earnestly protested unto your fathers in the day that I brought them up out of the land of Egypt, even unto this day, rising early and protesting, saying, Obey my voice. Yet they obeyed not, nor inclined their ear, but walked every one in the imagination of their evil heart: therefore I will bring upon them all the words of this covenant, which I commanded them to do: but they did them not.

High-Priest

The curs'd Word our enemy!

The Second Reading

High-Priest

A reading from the epistle of Paul to the Galatians:

A Member of the Cenobites

Wherefore then serveth the law? It was added because of transgressions, till the seed should come to whom the promise was made; and it was ordained by angels in the hand of a mediator. Now a mediator is not a mediator of one, but God is one. Is the law then against the promises of God? God forbid: for if there had been a law given which could have given life, verily righteousness should have been by the law. But the scripture hath concluded all under sin, that the promise by faith of Jesus Christ might be given to them that believe. But before faith came, we were kept under the law, shut up unto the faith which should afterwards be revealed. Wherefore the law was our schoolmaster to bring us unto Christ, that we might be justified by faith. Stand fast therefore in the liberty wherewith Christ hath made us free, and be not entangled again with the yoke of bondage. Behold, I Paul say unto you, that if ye be circumcised, Christ shall profit you nothing. For I testify again to every man that is circumcised, that he is a debtor to do the whole law. Christ is become of no effect unto you, whosoever of you are justified by the law; ye are fallen from grace. For we through the Spirit wait for the hope of righteousness by faith. For in Jesus Christ neither circumcision availeth any thing, nor uncircumcision; but faith which worketh by love.

HIGH-PRIEST

The curs'd Word our enemy!

The Reading of the Gospel

HIGH-PRIEST

A reading from the Curs'd Gospel according to Matthew: Think not that I am come to destroy the law, or the prophets: I am not come to destroy, but to fulfil. For verily I say unto you, Till heaven and earth pass, one jot or one tittle shall in no wise pass from the law, till all be fulfilled. Whosoever therefore shall break one of these least commandments, and shall teach men so, he shall be called the least in the kingdom of heaven: but whosoever shall do and teach them, the same shall be called great in the kingdom of heaven. For I say unto you, That except your righteousness shall exceed the righteousness of the scribes and Pharisees, ye shall in no case enter into the kingdom of heaven.

Legion of CENOBITES

Curs'd be the Word of God.

HIGH-PRIEST

All glory to thee, O Satan. All praise
To thee, O Satan. May the curses of
This Gospel tattoos our sins upon
Our foreheads in the curs'd Mark of the Beast.

Readings on Wickedness

The First Reading

HIGH-PRIEST

A reading from the book of Job:

A *Member of the* CENOBITES

Moreover Job continued his parable, and said, As God liveth, who hath taken away
my judgment; and the Almighty, who hath vexed my soul; All the while my breath is
in me, and the spirit of God is in my nostrils; My lips shall not speak wickedness, nor
my tongue utter deceit. God forbid that I should justify you: till I die I will not remove
mine integrity from me. My righteousness I hold fast, and will not let it go: my heart
shall not reproach me so long as I live. Let mine enemy be as the wicked, and he that
riseth up against me as the unrighteous. For what is the hope of the hypocrite, though
he hath gained, when God taketh away his soul? Will God hear his cry when trouble
cometh upon him? Will he delight himself in the Almighty? will he always call upon
God? I will teach you by the hand of God: that which is with the Almighty will I not
conceal. Behold, all ye yourselves have seen it; why then are ye thus altogether vain?
This is the portion of a wicked man with God, and the heritage of oppressors, which
they shall receive of the Almighty. If his children be multiplied, it is for the sword:
and his offspring shall not be satisfied with bread. Those that remain of him shall be
buried in death: and his widows shall not weep. Though he heap up silver as the dust,
and prepare raiment as the clay; He may prepare it, but the just shall put it on, and
the innocent shall divide the silver. He buildeth his house as a moth, and as a booth
that the keeper maketh. The rich man shall lie down, but he shall not be gathered: he
openeth his eyes, and he is not. Terrors take hold on him as waters, a tempest stealeth
him away in the night. The east wind carrieth him away, and he departeth: and as a
storm hurleth him out of his place. For God shall cast upon him, and not spare: he
would fain flee out of his hand. Men shall clap their hands at him, and shall hiss him
out of his place.

HIGH-PRIEST

The curs'd Word our enemy!

The Second Reading

HIGH-PRIEST

A reading from the epistle of Paul to the Romans:

A *Member of the* CENOBITES

What advantage then hath the Jew? or what profit is there of circumcision? Much
every way: chiefly, because that unto them were committed the oracles of God. For
what if some did not believe? shall their unbelief make the faith of God without effect?
God forbid: yea, let God be true, but every man a liar; as it is written, That thou
mightest be justified in thy sayings, and mightest overcome when thou art judged.

But if our unrighteousness commend the righteousness of God, what shall we say? Is God unrighteous who taketh vengeance? (I speak as a man) God forbid: for then how shall God judge the world? For if the truth of God hath more abounded through my lie unto his glory; why yet am I also judged as a sinner? And not rather, (as we be slanderously reported, and as some affirm that we say,) Let us do evil, that good may come? whose damnation is just.

HIGH-PRIEST

The curs'd Word our enemy!

The Reading of the Gospel

HIGH-PRIEST

A reading from the Curs'd Gospel according to Matthew: Woe unto you, scribes and Pharisees, hypocrites! because ye build the tombs of the prophets, and garnish the sepulchres of the righteous, And say, If we had been in the days of our fathers, we would not have been partakers with them in the blood of the prophets. Wherefore ye be witnesses unto yourselves, that ye are the children of them which killed the prophets. Fill ye up then the measure of your fathers. Ye serpents, ye generation of vipers, how can ye escape the damnation of hell? Wherefore, behold, I send unto you prophets, and wise men, and scribes: and some of them ye shall kill and crucify; and some of them shall ye scourge in your synagogues, and persecute them from city to city: That upon you may come all the righteous blood shed upon the earth, from the blood of righteous Abel unto the blood of Zacharias son of Barachias, whom ye slew between the temple and the altar. Verily I say unto you, All these things shall come upon this generation. O Jerusalem, Jerusalem, thou that killest the prophets, and stonest them which are sent unto thee, how often would I have gathered thy children together, even as a hen gathereth her chickens under her wings, and ye would not! Behold, your house is left unto you desolate. For I say unto you, Ye shall not see me henceforth, till ye shall say, Blessed is he that cometh in the name of the Lord.

Legion of CENOBITES

Curs'd be the Word of God.

HIGH-PRIEST

All glory to thee, O Satan. All praise
To thee, O Satan. May the curses of
This Gospel tattoos our sins upon
Our foreheads in the curs'd Mark of the Beast.

Readings on Foolishness

The First Reading

HIGH-PRIEST

A reading from the book of Jeremiah:

A *Member of the* CENOBITES

For my people is foolish, they have not known me; they are sottish children, and they have none understanding: they are wise to do evil, but to do good they have no knowledge.

HIGH-PRIEST

The curs'd Word our enemy!

The Second Reading

HIGH-PRIEST

A reading from the first epistle of Paul to the Corinthians:

A *Member of the* CENOBITES

For the preaching of the cross is to them that perish foolishness; but unto us which are saved it is the power of God. For it is written, I will destroy the wisdom of the wise, and will bring to nothing the understanding of the prudent. Where is the wise? where is the scribe? where is the disputer of this world? hath not God made foolish the wisdom of this world? For after that in the wisdom of God the world by wisdom knew not God, it pleased God by the foolishness of preaching to save them that believe. For the Jews require a sign, and the Greeks seek after wisdom: But we preach Christ crucified, unto the Jews a stumbling block, and unto the Greeks foolishness; But unto them which are called, both Jews and Greeks, Christ the power of God, and the wisdom of God. Because the foolishness of God is wiser than men; and the weakness of God is stronger than men.

HIGH-PRIEST

The curs'd Word our enemy!

The Reading of the Gospel

HIGH-PRIEST

A reading from the Curs'd Gospel according to Matthew: Woe unto you, scribes and Pharisees, hypocrites! because ye build the tombs of the prophets, and garnish the sepulchres of the righteous, And say, If we had been in the days of our fathers, we would not have been partakers with them in the blood of the prophets. Wherefore ye be witnesses unto yourselves, that ye are the children of them which killed the prophets. Fill ye up then the measure of your fathers. Ye serpents, ye generation of vipers, how can ye escape the damnation of hell? Wherefore, behold, I send unto you prophets, and wise men, and scribes: and some of them ye shall kill and crucify; and some of them shall ye scourge in your synagogues, and persecute them from city to city: That upon you may come all the righteous blood shed upon the earth, from the blood of righteous Abel unto the blood of Zacharias son of Barachias, whom ye slew between the temple and the altar. Verily I say unto you, All these things shall come upon this generation. O Jerusalem, Jerusalem, thou that killest the prophets, and stonest them which are sent unto thee, how often would I have gathered thy children together, even as a hen gathereth her chickens under her wings, and ye would not! Behold, your house is left unto you desolate. For I say unto you, Ye shall not see me henceforth, till ye shall say, Blessed is he that cometh in the name of the Lord.

Legion of CENOBITES

Curs'd be the Word of God.

HIGH-PRIEST

All glory to thee, O Satan. All praise
To thee, O Satan. May the curses of
This Gospel tattoos our sins upon
Our foreheads in the curs'd Mark of the Beast.

Readings on Drunkenness

The First Reading

HIGH-PRIEST

A reading from the book of Genesis:

A Member of the CENOBITES

And Lot went up out of Zoar, and dwelt in the mountain, and his two daughters with him; for he feared to dwell in Zoar: and he dwelt in a cave, he and his two daughters. And the firstborn said unto the younger, Our father is old, and there is not a man in the earth to come in unto us after the manner of all the earth: Come, let us make our father drink wine, and we will lie with him, that we may preserve seed of our father. And they made their father drink wine that night: and the firstborn went in, and lay with her father; and he perceived not when she lay down, nor when she arose. And it came to pass on the morrow, that the firstborn said unto the younger, Behold, I lay yesternight with my father: let us make him drink wine this night also; and go thou in, and lie with him, that we may preserve seed of our father. And they made their father drink wine that night also: and the younger arose, and lay with him; and he perceived not when she lay down, nor when she arose. Thus were both the daughters of Lot with child by their father. And the first born bare a son, and called his name Moab: the same is the father of the Moabites unto this day. And the younger, she also bare a son, and called his name Benammi: the same is the father of the children of Ammon unto this day.

HIGH-PRIEST

The curs'd Word our enemy!

The Second Reading

HIGH-PRIEST

A reading from the apocalypse of John to the Seven Churches:

A Member of the CENOBITES

And there came one of the seven angels which had the seven vials, and talked with me, saying unto me, Come hither; I will shew unto thee the judgment of the great whore that sitteth upon many waters: With whom the kings of the earth have committed fornication, and the inhabitants of the earth have been made drunk with the wine of her fornication. So he carried me away in the spirit into the wilderness: and I saw a woman sit upon a scarlet coloured beast, full of names of blasphemy, having seven heads and ten horns. And the woman was arrayed in purple and scarlet colour, and decked with gold and precious stones and pearls, having a golden cup in her hand full of abominations and filthiness of her fornication: And upon her forehead was a name written, Mystery, Babylon The Great, The Mother Of Harlots And Abominations Of The Earth. And I saw the woman drunken with the blood of the saints, and with the blood of the martyrs of Jesus: and when I saw her, I wondered with great admiration.

HIGH-PRIEST

The curs'd Word our enemy!

The Reading of the Gospel

HIGH-PRIEST

A reading from the Curs'd Gospel according to Luke: And when the messengers of John were departed, he began to speak unto the people concerning John, What went ye out into the wilderness for to see? A reed shaken with the wind? But what went ye out for to see? A man clothed in soft raiment? Behold, they which are gorgeously apparelled, and live delicately, are in kings' courts. But what went ye out for to see? A prophet? Yea, I say unto you, and much more than a prophet. This is he, of whom it is written, Behold, I send my messenger before thy face, which shall prepare thy way before thee. For I say unto you, Among those that are born of women there is not a greater prophet than John the Baptist: but he that is least in the kingdom of God is greater than he. For John the Baptist came neither eating bread nor drinking wine; and ye say, He hath a devil. The Son of man is come eating and drinking; and ye say, Behold a gluttonous man, and a winebibber, a friend of publicans and sinners! But wisdom is justified of all her children.

Legion of CENOBITES

Curs'd be the Word of God.

HIGH-PRIEST

All glory to thee, O Satan. All praise
To thee, O Satan. May the curses of
This Gospel tattoos our sins upon
Our foreheads in the curs'd Mark of the Beast.

Readings on Lord's Name in Vain

The First Reading

HIGH-PRIEST

A reading from the book of Ezekiel:

A *Member of the* CENOBITES

I wrought for my name's sake, that it should not be polluted before the heathen, among whom they were, in whose sight I made myself known unto them, in bringing them forth out of the land of Egypt. Wherefore I caused them to go forth out of the land of Egypt, and brought them into the wilderness. And I gave them my statutes, and shewed them my judgments, which if a man do, he shall even live in them. Moreover also I gave them my sabbaths, to be a sign between me and them, that they might know that I am the Lord that sanctify them. But the house of Israel rebelled against me in the wilderness: they walked not in my statutes, and they despised my judgments, which if a man do, he shall even live in them; and my sabbaths they greatly polluted: then I said, I would pour out my fury upon them in the wilderness, to consume them. But I wrought for my name's sake, that it should not be polluted before the heathen, in whose sight I brought them out. Yet also I lifted up my hand unto them in the wilderness, that I would not bring them into the land which I had given them, flowing with milk and honey, which is the glory of all lands; Because they despised my judgments, and walked not in my statutes, but polluted my sabbaths: for their heart went after their idols. Nevertheless mine eye spared them from destroying them, neither did I make an end of them in the wilderness. But I said unto their children in the wilderness, Walk ye not in the statutes of your fathers, neither observe their judgments, nor defile yourselves with their idols: I am the Lord your God; walk in my statutes, and keep my judgments, and do them; And hallow my sabbaths; and they shall be a sign between me and you, that ye may know that I am the Lord your God.

HIGH-PRIEST

The curs'd Word our enemy!

The Second Reading

HIGH-PRIEST

A continuation of the reading from the book of Ezekiel:

A *Member of the* CENOBITES

Notwithstanding the children rebelled against me: they walked not in my statutes, neither kept my judgments to do them, which if a man do, he shall even live in them; they polluted my sabbaths: then I said, I would pour out my fury upon them, to accomplish my anger against them in the wilderness. Nevertheless I withdrew mine hand, and wrought for my name's sake, that it should not be polluted in the sight of the heathen, in whose sight I brought them forth. I lifted up mine hand unto them also in the wilderness, that I would scatter them among the heathen, and disperse them through the countries; Because they had not executed my judgments, but had despised my statutes, and had polluted my sabbaths, and their eyes were after their fathers' idols. Wherefore I gave them also statutes that were not good, and judgments whereby they should not live; And I polluted them in their own gifts, in that they caused to pass through the fire all that openeth the womb, that I might make them desolate, to the end that they might know that I am the Lord.

HIGH-PRIEST

The curs'd Word our enemy!

The Reading of the Gospel

HIGH-PRIEST

A reading from the Curs'd Gospel according to John: the Jews round about him, and said unto him, How long dost thou make us to doubt? If thou be the Christ, tell us plainly. Jesus answered them, I told you, and ye believed not: the works that I do in my Father's name, they bear witness of me. But ye believe not, because ye are not of my sheep, as I said unto you. My sheep hear my voice, and I know them, and they follow me: And I give unto them eternal life; and they shall never perish, neither shall any man pluck them out of my hand. My Father, which gave them me, is greater than all; and no man is able to pluck them out of my Father's hand. I and my Father are one. Then the Jews took up stones again to stone him. Jesus answered them, Many good works have I shewed you from my Father; for which of those works do ye stone me? The Jews answered him, saying, For a good work we stone thee not; but for blasphemy; and because that thou, being a man, makest thyself God. Jesus answered them, Is it not written in your law, I said, Ye are gods? If he called them gods, unto whom the word of God came, and the scripture cannot be broken; Say ye of him, whom the Father hath sanctified, and sent into the world, Thou blasphemest; because I said, I am the Son of God? If I do not the works of my Father, believe me not. But if I do, though ye believe not me, believe the works: that ye may know, and believe, that the Father is in me, and I in him. Therefore they sought again to take him: but he escaped out of their hand.

Legion of CENOBITES

Curs'd be the Word of God.

HIGH-PRIEST

All glory to thee, O Satan. All praise
To thee, O Satan. May the curses of
This Gospel tattoos our sins upon
Our foreheads in the curs'd Mark of the Beast.

Readings on Blasphemy

The First Reading

HIGH-PRIEST

A reading from the book of Revelation:

A Member of the CENOBITES

And I stood upon the sand of the sea, and saw a beast rise up out of the sea, having seven heads and ten horns, and upon his horns ten crowns, and upon his heads the name of blasphemy. And the beast which I saw was like unto a leopard, and his feet were as the feet of a bear, and his mouth as the mouth of a lion: and the dragon gave him his power, and his seat, and great authority. And I saw one of his heads as it were wounded to death; and his deadly wound was healed: and all the world wondered after the beast. And they worshipped the dragon which gave power unto the beast: and they worshipped the beast, saying, Who is like unto the beast? who is able to make war with him? And there was given unto him a mouth speaking great things and blasphemies; and power was given unto him to continue forty and two months. And he opened his mouth in blasphemy against God, to blaspheme his name, and his tabernacle, and them that dwell in heaven. And it was given unto him to make war with the saints, and to overcome them: and power was given him over all kindreds, and tongues, and nations. And all that dwell upon the earth shall worship him, whose names are not written in the book of life of the Lamb slain from the foundation of the world. If any man have an ear, let him hear. He that leadeth into captivity shall go into captivity: he that killeth with the sword must be killed with the sword. Here is the patience and the faith of the saints.

HIGH-PRIEST

The curs'd Word our enemy!

The Second Reading

HIGH-PRIEST

A reading from the first epistle of Paul to Timothy:

A Member of the CENOBITES

And I thank Christ Jesus our Lord, who hath enabled me, for that he counted me faithful, putting me into the ministry; Who was before a blasphemer, and a persecutor, and injurious: but I obtained mercy, because I did it ignorantly in unbelief. And the grace of our Lord was exceeding abundant with faith and love which is in Christ Jesus. This is a faithful saying, and worthy of all acceptation, that Christ Jesus came into the world to save sinners; of whom I am chief. Howbeit for this cause I obtained mercy, that in me first Jesus Christ might shew forth all longsuffering, for a pattern to them which should hereafter believe on him to life everlasting. Now unto the King eternal, immortal, invisible, the only wise God, be honour and glory for ever and ever. Amen.

HIGH-PRIEST

The curs'd Word our enemy!

The Reading of the Gospel

HIGH-PRIEST

A reading from the Curs'd Gospel according to Matthew: Then was brought unto him one possessed with a devil, blind, and dumb: and he healed him, insomuch that the blind and dumb both spake and saw. And all the people were amazed, and said, Is not this the son of David? But when the Pharisees heard it, they said, This fellow doth not cast out devils, but by Beelzebub the prince of the devils. And Jesus knew their thoughts, and said unto them, Every kingdom divided against itself is brought to desolation; and every city or house divided against itself shall not stand: And if Satan cast out Satan, he is divided against himself; how shall then his kingdom stand? And if I by Beelzebub cast out devils, by whom do your children cast them out? therefore they shall be your judges. But if I cast out devils by the Spirit of God, then the kingdom of God is come unto you. Or else how can one enter into a strong man's house, and spoil his goods, except he first bind the strong man? and then he will spoil his house. He that is not with me is against me; and he that gathereth not with me scattereth abroad. Wherefore I say unto you, All manner of sin and blasphemy shall be forgiven unto men: but the blasphemy against the Holy Ghost shall not be forgiven unto men. And whosoever speaketh a word against the Son of man, it shall be forgiven him: but whosoever speaketh against the Holy Ghost, it shall not be forgiven him, neither in this world, neither in the world to come. Either make the tree good, and his fruit good; or else make the tree corrupt, and his fruit corrupt: for the tree is known by his fruit. O generation of vipers, how can ye, being evil, speak good things? for out of the abundance of the heart the mouth speaketh. A good man out of the good treasure of the heart bringeth forth good things: and an evil man out of the evil treasure bringeth forth evil things. But I say unto you, That every idle word that men shall speak, they shall give account thereof in the day of judgment. For by thy words thou shalt be justified, and by thy words thou shalt be condemned.

Legion of CENOBITES

Curs'd be the Word of God.

HIGH-PRIEST

All glory to thee, O Satan. All praise
To thee, O Satan. May the curses of
This Gospel tattoos our sins upon
Our foreheads in the curs'd Mark of the Beast.

The Rite of Desecration
(Anti-Baptism)
Part First - Outside the Grotto

The Questioning

HIGH-PRIEST

What asketh ye of the god of this world?

The CENOBITE/ADVOCATE [*Chooses any of the following or "Everything":*]

(1) Abuse (2) Aggression (3) Ambition (4) Anger (5) Arrogance (6) Baseness (7) Blasphemy (8) Calculation (9) Callousness (10) Capriciousness (11) Censoriousness (12) Conceitedness (13) Contempt (14) Cruelty (15) Cursing (16) Debasement (17) Deceit (18) Deception (19) Delusion (20) Derision (21) Desire for fame (22) Dipsomania (23) Discord (24) Disrespect (25) Disrespectfulness (26) Dissatisfaction (27) Dogmatism (28) Dominance (29) Eagerness for power (30) Effrontery (31) Egoism (32) Enviousness (33) Envy (34) Excessiveness (35) Faithlessness (36) Falseness (37) Furtiveness (38) Gambling (39) Garrulity (40) Gluttony (41) Greed (42) Greed for money (43) Grudge (44) Hard-heartedness (45) Hatred (46) Haughtiness (47) High-handedness (48) Hostility (49) Humiliation (50) Hurt (51) Hypocrisy (52) Ignorance (53) Imperiousness (54) Imposture (55) Impudence (56) Inattentiveness (57) Indifference (58) Ingratitude (59) Insatiability (60) Insidiousness (61) Intolerance (62) Intransigence (63) Irresponsibility (64) Jealousy (65) Know-it-all (66) Lack of comprehension (67) Lecherousness (68) Lying (69) Malignancy (70) Manipulation (71) Masochism (72) Mercilessness (73) Negativity (74) Obsession (75) Obstinacy (76) Obstinacy (77) Oppression (78) Ostentatiousness (79) Pessimism (80) Prejudice (81) Presumption (82) Pretence (83) Pride (84) Prodigality (85) Quarrelsomeness (86) Rage (87) Rapacity (88) Ridicule (89) Sadism (90) Sarcasm (91) Seducement (92) Self-denial (93) Self-hatred (94) Sexual lust (95) Shamelessness (96) Stinginess (97) Stubbornness (98) Torment (99) Tyranny (100) Unkindness (101)

Unruliness (102) Unyielding (103) Vanity (104) Vindictiveness (105)
Violence (106) Violent temper (107) Voluptuousness (108) Wrath

HIGH-PRIEST *(laughs heartily)*
> Not-a-thing shalt be bequeathed unto thee
> Freely! Must this be seized from he whom doth
> Possess it! Pray tell, if this be thy earthly
> Purpose, wherefore doth ye desire this?

The CENOBITE/ADVOCATE
> Ungodliness! And worldly desires!

HIGH-PRIEST
> If then you desire to enter into
> Desecration, keepeth this commandment:
> Do what thou wilt be the whole of the Law!

The Exsufflation

HIGH-PRIEST *(breathes 3 times on the Cenobite)*
> Commeth into him (her), most unclean spirit,
> And taketh the berth of the Holy Ghost!

The Mark of the Beast

HIGH-PRIEST *(draws three 6's on Cenobite's forehead)*
> The Beast causeth all, both small and great, rich
> And poor, free and bond, to receiveth a
> Mark in their right hand, or in their foreheads:
> Let him that hath understanding count the
> Number of the Beast: it is the number
> Of a man; his number is Six hundred
> Threescore and six. Receiveth the Mark of
> The Beast upon thy right hand; also upon
> Thy forehead; mayest thee reject the faith
> Of the heavenly Father. So order
> Thy life as to be, from henceforth led up
> Of the Spirit into the wilderness
> 'Part from God, tempted ye of the Devil!
> Let us pray: Mercilessly destroy the
> Christian we beseech thee, Infernal Lord;

And by thy infernal Will this Cenobite,
Signed with the number of the Beast,
By this first temptation he (she) Deserveth
Eternal damnation through Lord Satan!
The CENOBITE/ADVOCATE
    Shemhamphorasch!

The Imposition of Hands

HIGH-PRIEST (*with his hands, he seizes the Cenobite's head*)
    Let us pray: O! Unmerciful Satan,
    Father of Lies condemn this Cenobite,
    Whom thou hast most mercilessly condemned;
    Driveth out from him (her) all blindness of faith;
    Renounce the Atonement of Jesus Christ
    Wherewith he (she) hath been reconciled to God.
    Close unto him (her), O Satan, the gate of
    God's loving kindness, that being of sign
    Of weakness; that he (she) may wallow in the
    Foulness of all wicked desires, and
    In the sweet sweat of Thy precepts may he (she)
    Displease Christ in His Church, and may grow in
    Disgrace. Ne'er in Christ their Lord, their God.
The CENOBITE/ADVOCATE
    Shemhamphorasch!

The Imposition of Salt

HIGH-PRIEST (*puts a dash of salt in the Cenobite's mouth*)
    Receiveth the salt of doubt: let it be
    To thee a token of doubt so that ye
    Looketh back and becometh a pillar
    Of the salt of questioning, disbelief.
The CENOBITE/ADVOCATE
    Shemhamphorasch!
HIGH-PRIEST
    Mayest the Lord of Lies be with us all.

Legion of CENOBITES
 And with the spirit of domination.

HIGH-PRIEST
 Let us pray: O! Adversary of God,
 O! Satan, the Father of Lies, vouchsafe,
 That we looketh back from behind us and
 Becometh a pillar of the salt of
 Questioning. Lead him (her) so that ye maketh
 Their Father drink wine, and lieth with him,
 That ye preserve the seed of thy Father.
 Thus shalt our daughters be with child of their
 Father, that together with thy faithful,
 Mayest deserve damnation Eternal.

The CENOBITE/ADVOCATE
 Shemhamphorasch!

Part Second - Admission to the Grotto

The Possession

HIGH-PRIEST (*draws three 6's on Cenobite's forehead*)
 I invite thee, unclean spirit, in the
 Name of Satan, Father of Lies, Prince of
 Darkness, and the Bloody Menses, that thou
 Come in and desecrate this Creation
 Of the Lord God of Israel. Renounce
 His Misborn Son's Atonement. And deny
 The saving grace of the Holy Spirit.
 For Christ rejects thee, O! accursed one, Who
 The Jews did persecute, and sought to slay
 Him, because he had done these things on the
 Sabbath day. Therefore accursed devil,
 Desecrate this soul, giving no honor
 To the Dead and False God; and giveth no
 Honor to Jesus Christ His Misborn Son;
 And giveth none to the Holy Spirit;
 Mayest they depart from this Cenobite

Of Satan because their God and their Lord
Jesus Christ hath condemned him (her) to Hellfire
In this disgraced font of Desecration.

The Mark of the Beast

HIGH-PRIEST (*again draws three 6's on Cenobite's forehead*)
And this Mark of the Beast, which we make 'on
His (her) forehead; Jesus Christ, the Misborn Son
Of God, ne'er darest thou violate with
Thy sanctimonious morality.
The CENOBITE/ADVOCATE
Shemhamphorasch!

The Imposition of Hands

HIGH-PRIEST (*again, with his hands, he seizes the Cenobite's head*)
Let us pray: O Infernal One, Father
Of Lies, Eternally damned, bringer of
Darkness, we renounce God's everlasting
And most just goodness. We implore thou wouldst
Vouchsafe to deceive him (her) with the darkness
Of thy truth and enlighten him (her), giveth
Unto him (her), true knowledge! Knowledge of the
Tree of Good and Evil! that being made
Worthy of Eternal Damnation of
The Thy Desecration, he (she) may hold hate,
False counsel, and thy unholy doctrine.
Through O! ruthless Satan, our Infernal Lord.
The CENOBITE/ADVOCATE
Shemhamphorasch!

The Admission to the Grotto

HIGH-PRIEST
Abandon all Hope, you who enter here!
The CENOBITE/ADVOCATE
Shemhamphorasch!

The Dionicean Creed and Pater

HIGH-PRIEST

I praise Mighty and Merciless Satan,
The Father of Lies, O! despoiler of
Heaven and earth. Despoiler of all things,
Visible and invisible. I praise
The Prince of Darkness, the Son of Satan,
One of the many born of the Father
Throughout all ages. Darkness of Darkness.
False God of False Gods. Made not begotten.
Never in substance with God the Father,
Through whom all things are damned. Who for us men
And for our damnation, he rose up from
The pits of Hell. By the vulgar power
Of the Hounds of Hell, was born of Lilith
The Lustful and became a dæmon.
He was betrayed by his own Creator,
He suffered and was cast into the pits
Of Hell. From the eighth day of Creation
Until its End. In fulfillment of the
Scriptures. He fell from Heaven and into
Hell descended, and is seated at the
Left hand of the Father of Lies. And he
Will come again in damnation, to rule
The living and the dead, And his kingdom
There hath seen no end. O! I believe in
The Hounds of Hell, the Prince of Darkness,
The taker of life, who recedes with the
Father of Lies and the Prince of Darkness.
With the Father and the Prince, Satan is
Worshipped and glorified. In one unholy,
Blasphemous and Satanic church. We praise
No baptism for the remission of
Glorious sin. I expect the defeat of
God in the coming war, the damnation in

Hell to come. I rebuke the one false God,
The Father, the Impotent, Creator
Of Heaven and Hell, and of all the things,
Importunate and insignificant.
I rebuke the Bastard, Jesus the Christ,
The only Son of God, eternally
Perverted of the Father, God but not
God, Light but Darkness, False God from False God
Created not begotten, nary in
Being with the Father. Though him all things
Are damned. For us men, for our damnation,
He rose from the pits of Hell By the lusts
Of the Holy Whoremonger, He spewed forth
From of the cunt of Mary the Virgin
Whore like unto vomit and was born man.
For his cenobites' damnation shalt He
Be crucified by the Jews' pawn Pilate;
He shalt suffer the agony of our father
He shalt die not unlike a mongrel dog.
Shalt be buried a' stolen from the grave
By his Disciples and away hidden.
On the Third day he creeps from the shadows,
In nullification of the Scriptures.
Flee to the green pastures of England where
He propagates the Line of David.
His heirs will come again, in condemnation,
To rule the living and demean the dead.
And the Church will come to a fitting end.
Yeah! I rebuke the Holy Whoremonger,
Their Lord, the thief of Life, who recedes from
The Father and from the Bastard Son.
With the Father and the Bastard Son
And He is worshipped in idolatry.
He hast born false witness through the Prophets.
Yeah! We doth rebuke the one holy and
Apostolic Church. Yeah! we rebuke one

Baptism for the forgiveness of sins.
We curse the resurrection of the dead
For no life abides in the world to come.
    Shemhamphorasch!
Our Master who art in Hell,
Damned be thy name.
Through the halls of Heaven and Earth,
Banished to thy kingdom of Hellfire and Brimstone.
Give us this night, our ritual sacrifices;
And grant us our Indulgences,
As we trespass against those who trespass against us.
Lead us into Divine Temptation,
And deliver us into Evil.
    Shemhamphorasch!

Part Third - Before the Altar of Flesh

The Joyful Possession

HIGH-PRIEST

    I invite thee, unclean spirit, in the
    Name of Satan, Father of Lies, Prince of
    Darkness, and the Bloody Menses, that thou
    Come in and desecrate this Creation
    Of the Lord God of Israel. Renounce
    His Misborn Son's Atonement. And deny
    The saving grace of the Holy Spirit.
    Therefore accursed devil desecrate
    This creature of God, whom their Lord hath deigned
    To call unto His most holy temple,
    That it had been made the temple of the
    Living God, and that the Holy Spirit
    Be cast e'er out. Profane the Christ their Lord,
    Who shall come to judge the living and the
    Dead, and the world by fire of Judgment Day.

The Quid Nobis et Tibi

HIGH-PRIEST

> Let us alone; what have we to do with
> Thee, thou Jesus of Nazareth? Art thou
> Come to destroy us? I know thee who thou
> Art, the Holy One of God the Father!

The Renunciation of Jesus

HIGH-PRIEST

> (Name), do you renounce Jesus the Christ?

The CENOBITE/ADVOCATE

> I do renounce him.

HIGH-PRIEST

> And all His works?

The CENOBITE/ADVOCATE

> I do renounce him.

HIGH-PRIEST

> And all his pomps?

The CENOBITE/ADVOCATE

> I do renounce him.

The Smearing

HIGH-PRIEST (*smears the Cenobite with the menses of a virgin*)

> I desecrate you with the menses of
> Damnation, in Satan, Infernal Lord,
> That you may have Eternal Damnation.

The CENOBITE/ADVOCATE

> > Shemhamphorasch!

Part Fourth - Before the Font

The Profession of Doubt

HIGH-PRIEST

> (Name), do you believe in God the Father Almighty, Creator of Heaven
> and Earth?

184

The Cenobite/Advocate

I believe not.

High-Priest

Do you believe in Jesus Christ, His only Son their Lord, Who was born and Who suffered?

The Cenobite/Advocate

I believe not.

High-Priest

Do you believe in the Holy Ghost, the Holy Catholic Church, the communion of Saints, the forgiveness of sins, the resurrection of the body and life everlasting?

The Cenobite/Advocate

I believe not.

High-Priest

(Name), do you believe in Satan, your father the devil, and the lusts of your father? He was a murderer from the beginning, and abode not in the truth, because there is no truth in him. When he speaketh a lie, he speaketh of his own: for he is a liar, and the father of it.

The Cenobite/Advocate

I do believe.

High-Priest

Do you believe in the Prince of Darkness, the rulers, the authorities, the world powers of this darkness, the spiritual forces of evil in the heavens?

The Cenobite/Advocate

I do believe.

High-Priest

Do you believe in the Bloody Menses, the altar of flesh, young, virginal, menstruating, and pure, the Number of the Beast, the Church of Eternal Damnation, the ridiculousness of Atonement, the decomposition of the dead, and damnation Eternal.

The Cenobite/Advocate

I do believe.

The Desecration

High-Priest

Wilt you receiveth the desecration?

The CENOBITE/ADVOCATE
>I will!

HIGH-PRIEST (*pours three shots of grain alcohol over the head of the Cenobite*)
>I desecrate you, defile you, wound you,
>In the Name of Satan, Father of Lies,
>Prince of Darkness, and the Bloody Menses.

The Smearing of Bloody Menses

HIGH-PRIEST (*again, smears the Cenobite with the menses of a virgin*)
>May Merciless Satan, the Father of
>Lies, who desecrates thee with the Bloody
>Menses, and who hath given unto thee
>The furtherance of thy sins, and may he
>Himself defile thee with Bloody Menses
>Of desecration; the defilement
>In the Name of Satan, Father of Lies,
>Prince of Darkness, and the Bloody Menses.

The CENOBITE/ADVOCATE
>Shemhamphorasch!

HIGH-PRIEST
>Mayest the Lord of Lies be with us all.

Legion of CENOBITES
>And with the spirit of domination.

The White Bloody Napkin

HIGH-PRIEST (*takes a soiled sanitary napkin and places it on the head of the Cenobite*)
>Receiveth this defiled, bloody garment,
>Which mayest thou carry stained before the
>Suffering throne of our Infernal Lord,
>That thou may have damnation Eternal.

The Extinguished Candle

HIGH-PRIEST (*gives the Cenobite a recently extinguished candle*)
>Receiveth this extinguished light and keep
>Thy Desecration, so as to be with

Blame fore'er: keepeth not the commandments
Of God, that upon the day of Jugdment
Thy mayest not meet Him together with
All of the Saints in the Heavenly court,
And mayest have damnation Eternal,
And suffer thee for ever and ever.

The CENOBITE/ADVOCATE

Shemhamphorasch!

The Last Words

HIGH-PRIEST

Go in animosity! may their Lord
Condemn thee to damnation Eternal.

The CENOBITE/ADVOCATE

Shemhamphorasch!

www.ingramcontent.com/pod-product-compliance
Lightning Source LLC
LaVergne TN
LVHW051235080426
835513LV00016B/1593